ESSE...
BOOK THREE

ESSENTIAL ENGLISH

for
Foreign Students
BOOK THREE

revised edition

by

C. E. ECKERSLEY

Illustrations by
CHARLES SALISBURY,
BURGESS SHARROCKS,
PORTEOUS WOOD
and from 'Punch' and 'Woman's Journal'

LONGMAN

LONGMAN GROUP LIMITED
London

*Associated companies, branches and representatives
throughout the world*

First published 1941
Revised edition 1945
Revised edition 1956
New impressions *1958; *1959; *1961; *1962; *1963;
*1964; *1965 (twice); *July 1966; *January 1968;
*June, *October 1969; *December 1970;
*March 1972; 1974; 1975;
1977; *1979 (twice); 1980

ISBN 0 582 52018 5

Printed in Hong Kong by
Wing Tai Cheung Printing Co Ltd

PREFACE

ESSENTIAL ENGLISH is a course in four books, of which this is the third, for the teaching of English to adult foreign students. It aims at giving the student a sound k nowledge of the essentials of both spoken and written English and taking him well on the way to a mastery of idiomatic conversational and literary English.

The normal constructions and sentence patterns of English are introduced gradually and systematically, and are well drilled at every stage. The learner is guided through "essential" grammar in the simplest possible manner, and every new construction is explained and illustrated as soon as it is used.

The restricted vocabulary within which the four books are written has been based on *A General Service List of English Words*.[1] But neither this list, nor any other list, has been followed slavishly and blindly; the vocabulary and the grammar and the structures taught have been tested constantly by the experience gained during some thirty years of teaching English to foreign students or writing text-books for them.

Because I believe that a knowledge of the *spoken* tongue is the true basis of language learning, much of this book is in "conversational" form; and my constant endeavour has been to ensure that, despite the restrictions that a limited vocabulary naturally imposes, every sentence in these conversations is expressed in the living colloquial idiom that an educated Englishman would use.

And, since the most effective spur to learning a language (or anything else) is interest, every effort has been made to cover the linguistic pill with the jam of gaiety. So, as soon as the preliminaries are mastered, the reader is introduced to Mr. Priestley, his household and his group of students. We see them here and in all the other books chatting together, telling jokes, reading stories that they have written, singing songs or acting short plays. It is on these conversations and stories and the "talks by Mr. Priestley" that the language teaching is based, and from them that the copious exercises by which the teacher is enabled to test how far the work has been understood, are drawn.

There are numerous changes in this new edition. Fresh, and it is hoped, more interesting reading material has been added,

[1] A new edition of the *Interim Report on Vocabulary Selection* (Longmans).

including two short plays, some further glimpses into the home-life of the Priestleys—including Mr. Priestley's ill-fated attempt to erect a hen-house—the story of yet another of Hob's extraordinary relatives and a story by Lucille. One objection that had been raised against the material in the earlier edition of *Essential English* was that the scene was almost entirely in London. So, in Book III we send some of our characters on a trip to Stratford, Olaf pays a visit to Oxford and gets a very full account from John Priestley of Oxford, past and present, and Frieda and Jan write about their holiday in Wales. Another innovation is the inclusion of a "hand-ful of poems", simple enough for students at this stage and yet containing one or two of the supreme lyrics of the language.

In the language work grammar—the "essential" grammar—is dealt with systematically, particular attention being given to the "Special" Verbs (the Anomalous Finites). Other new features are three new "Stories Without Words" (pages 15, 81, 150), a chapter on Punctuation, the fuller treatment of Conditional Sentences and *should* and *would*, and an Index. And, as the pupils are now sufficiently advanced to do "unseen" dictation, the Dictation Exercises—though still based on the lesson where they appear and still containing only those words and constructions that have already been taught—are now transferred to the Teacher's hand-book [1] that has been prepared to accompany this volume. In this Teacher's Book further guidance has been given on the main techniques of language teaching, a great deal of extra teaching material and linguistic information has been given in the "Com-mentaries", detailed suggestions and practical hints are given on the teaching of each lesson, and a complete Key to the exercises in the Pupil's Book is provided.

Though a text-book that is the ideal one to every teacher and student is, perhaps, an impossibility, it is hoped that most students and teachers will feel that this new edition is an im-provement on the old one, but the author will be most grateful at any time for further criticisms and suggestions that will help to make ESSENTIAL ENGLISH more useful to those who study it or teach from it.

C. E. E.

---

[1] *Essential English, Book III, Teacher's Book.*

CONTENTS

vii

ESSENTIAL ENGLISH
BOOK THREE
TEACHER'S BOOK
with
Teaching notes, additional lesson
material, Dictation Exercises and
a Key to all the Exercises

ACKNOWLEDGEMENTS

We are indebted to the following for permission to quote copyright
material:

Mrs. Frances Cornford and The Cresset Press Ltd. for *To A Fat Lady Seen
from The Train*; Mrs. H. M. Davies for "Leisure" from *The Collected
Poems of W. H. Davies*, published by Messrs. Jonathan Cape Ltd.; the
author's widow and Messrs. J. M. Dent & Sons Ltd. for *To a Poet A
Thousand Years Hence* by James Elroy Flecker; and The Society of
Authors as the literary representative of the Trustees of the estate of the
late A. E. Housman, Messrs. Jonathan Cape Ltd. (publishers of A. E.
Housman's *Collected Poems*) and Messrs. Henry Holt and Co. Inc. for
"Loveliest of Trees" from *A Shropshire Lad* (copyright 1924 by Henry
Holt and Co. Inc.); and Messrs. T. Werner Laurie Ltd. for extracts from
Biography for Beginners by E. C. Bentley.

LESSON 1

Hob Gives His First Impressions of England

[*The students whom we have met in Books I and II,*
LUCILLE, FRIEDA, OLAF, JAN, PEDRO *and* HOB, *are
back again with* MR. PRIESTLEY, *their teacher, in his
study.*]

HOB: Do you remember, sir, that at our last lesson
before the holidays, you promised to let me tell
the story of my first day in England?

MR. PRIESTLEY: I remember it very well; and so now,
at our very first lesson, we are all waiting to hear
what you have to tell us.

HOB: Thank you, sir. Well, my first impressions of
England are connected with food——

LUCILLE: You don't need to tell us that!

HOB: ...and, strange to say, they are of how an
English breakfast beat me.

FRIEDA: You don't really expect us to believe that, do
you, Hob?

HOB: Well, it's quite true. Of course, it was some time
ago and, though I say it myself, I'm a better man
now than I was then, but, honestly, I was beaten.
But let me begin at the beginning.

* * * *

When I left the train at Victoria Station my first impression was of rain and fog and people with umbrellas. A taxi-cab, which might have been used by Lot and his family as they left Sodom and Gomorrah, took me and my luggage and struggled bravely through the traffic. And what traffic and what crowds! I had never believed my geography teacher when he told us there were more people in London than in the whole of my country. I thought he had just said it to make his lesson more interesting, but I believed him now.

However, I got to my little hotel at last, and the first thing that took my eye was the porter, a big fat man with a round pink face like an advertisement for babies' food. Then I met the manager. He rubbed his hands all the time as if he was washing them, and smiled without stopping. What he said I could not understand, though I had learned English at school. I said to

myself, "Perhaps he doesn't speak it very well—
some English people don't." But I told him my
name, and he smiled again and told one of the
little boys with brass buttons to show me up to
my room. Ten minutes later I was lying in a hot
bath washing off the last dusty reminders of the
Continent; another ten minutes and I was under
the bedclothes and fast asleep.

When I woke next morning, I felt hungrier
than I had ever felt in my life before; I seemed
to have a hole instead of a stomach. I dressed
quickly and hurried down to the dining-room.
It was a big room with six tall windows and the
ugliest wallpaper I had ever seen. However, I
had been told that the hotel was not beautiful but
that you were better fed there than in any other
hotel in London;—and that was what I wanted
just then.

The waiter came hurrying up. Before I came
downstairs I had prepared myself very carefully
for what I must say. I had looked three times in
my dictionary to make sure that "breakfast"
really meant "breakfast". I had tried to get the
right pronunciation and had stood in front of a
mirror and twisted my mouth until it ached.

The waiter asked me something I could not
understand, but I spoke only my one prepared
word, "BREAKFAST". He looked at me in a
puzzled way, so I repeated it. Still he did not
understand. It was unbelievable that English
people didn't understand their own language.
The waiter shook his head, bowed and went

away, but he came back in a minute and brought the manager with him. I was feeling slightly annoyed, but I said, "BREAKFAST". The manager smiled and washed his hands, but looked as helpless as the waiter, so I took out a pencil and wrote on the table napkin, "Breakfast". I have never seen such surprised faces in my life—so perhaps I did not pronounce it correctly after all.

A little later the waiter brought a tray with tea, toast, butter and marmalade—enough to feed a small army—and went away. But I was hungry, and I left nothing; I am sure I drank at least two pints of tea, ate almost a loaf of toasted bread and large quantities of butter and marmalade with it. When the waiter came back I thought his face showed a little surprise, but you can never tell what a waiter's face really shows. In another minute he brought another tray with a huge portion of bacon and eggs. He must have misunderstood me, but I thought it was no use explaining to people who don't understand their own language, so I just set to work on the bacon and eggs and ate on steadily, wondering all the time whether I could possibly clear that plate.

Well, I finished the bacon and eggs, and was just trying to get up out of the chair when here was the waiter again with another tray. This time it was a whole fish in a thick white sauce. Surely this must be a joke, I thought; but before I could tell him anything, he had put down the tray and gone away. There was nothing for it but to face that fish with what little courage I had left, but all the time I was eating it I was trying to think of what I could say to that waiter when he returned. I had brought my grammar book with me in case of need, but have you noticed how all these grammar books give you sentences like this:

The little girl gave the pen of my aunt to the gardener.

—but not the *essential* English about breakfasts big enough to feed an army?

But at last I had made up two sentences in my mind—avoiding verbs as much as possible, because I was never sure which were irregular. I called the waiter to me. He bowed, and then I told him in very correct English what I thought of English breakfasts. I told him that only a man who was dying of hunger could eat such a breakfast. He must have understood me at once. I felt very proud of my English, especially " dying of hunger "; that was a grand expression. I have never seen anyone clear away the empty plates as fast as he did; he almost ran out of the room, but in a minute he was back again—with a big plateful of sandwiches. This was too much. I gave up the struggle. I got up and made my way slowly and heavily to my room—at least five pounds heavier. I never believed until then that any meal could defeat me, but on that day I met my Waterloo.[1]

[1] To meet one's Waterloo = to be completely defeated. Napoleon was defeated at Waterloo in 1815.

EXERCISES

(Exercises II–VII in this lesson are planned to revise the grammar taught in Book II of *Essential English*.)

I. *Use the following words and phrases in sentences:*

1. expect	8. brass	15. in case of need
2. connected with	9. ugly	16. avoid
3. struggle	10. twist	17. dying of hunger
4. traffic	11. bow	18. big enough
5. dusty	12. loaf	19. defeat
6. umbrella	13. tray	20. marmalade
7. advertisement	14. burst	21. sauce

II. *In the following sentences put all the finite verbs into their corresponding past tense and give the name of each tense that you use:*

1. When I leave the train my impression is of rain and fog.
2. He takes my luggage and struggles through the traffic.
3. I have never believed my geography teacher; I think he has said that to make the lesson interesting.
4. The first thing that takes my eye is the porter.
5. I can't understand what he says.
6. He tells one of the little boys to show me to my room.
7. When I wake I feel hungry.
8. I have been told that you are well fed in this hotel.
9. I can't understand him, but I speak my prepared words.
10. He doesn't understand me.
11. I take out a pencil and write "breakfast".
12. Perhaps I do not pronounce it correctly.
13. The waiter brings in a tray with tea and toast, and goes away.
14. He misunderstands me.
15. I set to work on the bacon and eggs and eat steadily.
16. I am wondering whether I can clear the plate, or whether I shall burst.

17. I tell him that only a man who is dying of hunger can eat such a breakfast.
18. He almost runs out of the room.
19. I give up the struggle, and get up to make my way out.
20. I don't believe a meal can defeat me—but I meet my Waterloo.
21. I shall finish my breakfast by ten o'clock. (*Turn this verb into the Future Perfect Tense.*)

III. *Replace the words in italics in the following sentences by possessive pronouns:*

1. You told me your first impressions, now I will tell you *my first impressions.*
2. Those are my first impressions. What are *your first impressions?*
3. Your taxis look very old; *our taxis* are newer.
4. I shook my head, and the waiter shook *his head.*
5. In the breakfast-room of the hotel there were four people: a woman, her two small sons, and I. I ate my breakfast, she ate *her breakfast,* and the boys ate *their breakfast.*

IV. "I had prepared *myself* very carefully."
What kind of pronoun is myself? *Give the corresponding pronouns for* you (*singular*), him, her, you (*plural*), it, us, them. *Explain the difference in meaning between the sentences:*

1. He helped him.
2. He helped himself.

V. *What does* shall, will, *or* going to *express in each of the following sentences:*

1. Tell me what you want for breakfast and I *will* get it for you.

2. *Shall* I bring you some more sandwiches?
3. If you want more sandwiches you *shall* have them.
4. I *will* learn to speak English even if it takes me five years.
5. I *am going to* write a letter home tomorrow afternoon.
6. There are a lot of black clouds in the sky; I think it *is going to* rain.

VI. *What tense is used in the following sentences?*

1. I am sure Hob *won't be feeling* hungry after that breakfast.
2. This time tomorrow I *shall be flying* to Paris. What *will you be doing* then?

What is this tense used for?

VII. *What is the difference between a sentence with a verb in the Active Voice and a sentence with a verb in the Passive Voice?*

Turn the following from Active Voice to Passive Voice:

1. Mr. Priestley teaches the students.
2. A taxi-cab took me to my hotel.
3. In this hotel the manager meets all the new guests.
4. The waiter brings the breakfast.
5. The waiter brought the breakfast.
6. The waiter will bring the breakfast.
7. They feed you well at this hotel.
8. They speak English there, but not Ruritanian.
9. They will feed you well at this hotel.
10. They fed me well at that hotel.

Composition Exercises

1. Describe the adventure in the hotel as the waiter might have told it.
2. Write a short story of your own, ending "... but that day I met my Waterloo."

LESSON 2

Olaf and Pedro Discuss Their Plans

PEDRO: How much longer are you staying in England, Olaf?

OLAF: Well, I don't quite know, but I shall be here for another year at any rate, probably two years.

PEDRO: That's good. I shall be here for at least another year.

OLAF: What are you going to do when you leave Mr. Priestley's?

PEDRO: I want to go to Cambridge. I discussed all this with my father before I left home and he said that he wanted me to spend a year in Paris and a year in Germany so that I could get a really good knowledge of French and German. Then he wanted me to spend two or three years with Mr. Priestley and try for an English degree at Cambridge.

OLAF: Have you enjoyed your stay in England?

PEDRO: Oh yes, very much. I knew it would be pleasant but I didn't think I should meet such interesting people. But what are you going to do when you leave England?

OLAF: I am going into my father's business, a shipping company.

PEDRO: That will be very interesting.

OLAF: Yes, I think so. At first I didn't think it would and I wanted something quite different. I thought life in an office was very dull.

PEDRO: What did you want to do?

OLAF: I wanted to be an artist and paint pictures. I said that nothing would ever make me go into an office. "The only life for me," I said, "is a life of art. In a few years I shall earn fame and fortune by my pictures." Of course I was only fifteen or sixteen and hadn't much sense.

HOB: I painted a picture once. I showed it to an artist, Miguel Macasso, who had sold a picture to Uncle Albert, and do you know what he said about it? He said that my picture would hang in the British Museum long after Rubens and Rembrandt were forgotten.

OLAF: Did he really?

HOB: Yes. But he added, "But not until they are forgotten." Macasso was a funny fellow. I remember one time I was at his house and, as he looked through the window, he saw an old fisherman going by. Macasso thought the old man would make a good subject for a picture so he told me to go out and tell the fisherman that Mr. Macasso wanted to paint him. I went. The man thought about it for a minute or so and said, "What will he pay me?" I said that he would give him two pounds. The man still hesitated, so I said, "It's an easy way to earn two pounds." "Oh! I know that," said the man, "but I am wondering how I shall get the paint off afterwards."

PEDRO: To come back to your story, Olaf, what did your father say?

OLAF: Oh, he was very good about it. He said I could go to the best art teacher in Stockholm and have some lessons. Well, after a week or two the teacher told me that it was a waste of time for him to go on teaching me. "You will never be a painter," he said, "not if you live to be a hundred. Don't come for any more lessons. Go back to your office."

PEDRO: Well, that was honest enough, but rather hard on you.

OLAF: Oh, I didn't mind. I told him that I knew he was right.

PEDRO: So you went to your father's office then?

OLAF: Yes. My father was very pleased and said he wanted me to spend a year there to get a good knowledge of the organisation of the business. "At the end of a year," he said, "you can go to my friend, Mr. Priestley, to learn English well." You see, we do a lot of business with England. He added that when I knew English well, he would arrange for me to go into an English firm to learn English business methods.[1]

PEDRO: So I suppose that some day you will be managing a shipping business in Stockholm.

OLAF: Well, my father said that in nine or ten years' time he wanted to retire, and he hoped that by that time I should be able to run the business.

PEDRO: That sounds fine.

[1] You see him in this firm in *English Commercial Practice and Correspondence* (Longmans).

OLAF: Yes, I shall be very proud when I can write to you on paper headed:

> Gustav Petersen & *Son*,
> Shipping Agents,
> Stockholm

and say, "Come and spend a holiday with me in Sweden."

HOB: I must tell you another story about Miguel Macasso. One day a very wealthy American, Hiram Boost, came to Macasso—you may have heard of Boost, he's in films—and he said he had bought, secretly, a valuable 16th century "old master". He said, "I know that the English Government won't let me take it out of England, but I have a plan to get round that. I want you to paint a picture—it doesn't matter what it is— on top of the 'old master'." Hiram then explained that he could quite easily get Macasso's picture removed from the canvas when he got to New York, without damaging the painting underneath. Well, Macasso painted a picture of a London gas-works on it, and old Boost got the canvas to New York all right and sent it to the firm he knew to have Macasso's painting removed. About a week later he got a telegram from the firm. It said: "We have removed the picture of London gas-works, also 'old master', and are now down to a portrait of Queen Victoria. When do you want us to stop?"

EXERCISES

I. *Use each of the following words and phrases in sentences:*

1. at any rate
2. discuss
3. knowledge
4. degree
5. company
6. artist
7. fame
8. office
9. organisation
10. method
11. manage
12. firm
13. plan
14. damage
15. get round
16. remove
17. down to
18. portrait
19. arrange
20. fisherman

II. *Write questions to which the following are answers:*

1. I shall be here for another year.
2. I'm going to Cambridge.
3. Yes, I spent a year in Paris and a year in Germany.
4. So that I could get a good knowledge of the language and the people.
5. Oh, yes, I enjoyed it very much.
6. He has a shipping office.
7. Because I thought it would be a terribly dull business.
8. He asked the servant what the artist would pay him.
9. Because he was wondering how he would get the paint off afterwards.
10. Oh, they were very nice about it, and let me take lessons.
11. He thought I should never be a painter.
12. Because we do a lot of trade with England.
13. He says in nine or ten years.
14. Because he knew the Government wouldn't let him take it out of England.
15. It doesn't matter what the picture is.

III. *Arrange the following in the correct order:*

1. You in England are staying how much longer?
2. I here for another year shall be at any rate.
3. When you leave here to do what are you going?

4. Your stay here you have enjoyed?
5. With my father all this before I left home I discussed.
6. Pleasant it would be I knew, but such interesting people I should meet I didn't think.
7. How the paint I shall get off afterwards am I wondering.
8. A picture on top of the "old master" you to paint I want what is it it doesn't matter.
9. A telegram about a week later from the firm he got.
10. That my picture in the British Museum would hang he said after long were forgotten Rubens and Rembrandt.

IV. *Express in one word the meaning of each of the following phrases.* All the words required are in the lesson. You are given the first letter of each word and the number of letters in it.

1. trade and the getting of money (b – – – – – – –).
2. not interesting (d – – –).
3. a lot of money; wealth (f – – – – – –).
4. to make up one's mind (d – – – – –).
5. to be unable to make up one's mind (h – – – – – – –).
6. house or room used as a place of business (o – – – – –).
7. to give up one's work when one is old (r – – – – –).
8. to get pleasure from (e – – – –).
9. to have in mind, not to forget (r – – – – – – –).
10. arrangement so that all parts work together well (o – – – – – – – – – – –).

Composition Exercises

1. Tell or write the story (*a*) of the fisherman who didn't want to be painted, (*b*) of Hiram Boost's picture.
2. Tell or write the story of Olaf's life as he tells it to you here

THE BIRDS THAT LIKED MILK

Answer the following questions. These words will help you: *bag, bottle, fence, full, empty, beak, milkman.*

PICTURE 1. What is the woman carrying in her right hand? Where do you think she is going? Do you think she will be away from home for an hour or two or a day or two? What makes you think that? What is she holding in her left hand? What can you see near the door-step? Is that milk bottle full or empty?

PICTURE 2. Who are watching her? Where are the birds? Where is she putting the note? What do you think she has written on it? What has she done with her bag?

PICTURE 3. What is one of the birds doing? What is the other one doing?

PICTURE 4. What is the bird doing now? What is it carrying in its beak? How do you know that the bottle is empty? Has the artist made it clear to you?

PICTURE 5. What is this man? What is he carrying? How many bottles of milk has he left on the door-step? Is it a full bottle or an empty one? What has he done with the empty bottle? Where are the birds? What are they doing?

PICTURE 6. Where are the birds now? What are they doing? Why did they take away the note?

Hollowood

(Illustrations reproduced by permission of the Proprietors of "Punch")

Now tell (or write) the story of THE BIRDS THAT LIKED MILK.

LESSON 3

Direct and Indirect Speech (i)

We can often say in two different ways what some-one has said. We can give the exact words of the speaker, e.g.,

Pedro said: "I want to go to Cambridge."

This is **Direct** Speech.

On the other hand, instead of giving the exact words that Pedro said, we might report what Pedro said, like this:

Pedro said that he wanted to go to Cambridge.

This is **Indirect** or Reported Speech.

In Lesson 2 there are a number of examples of both forms. Here are one or two of them:

Direct	Indirect
1. "The only life for me is a life of art."	1. Olaf said that the only life for him was a life of art.
2. "It's an easy way to earn two pounds."	2. Hob said that it was an easy way to earn two pounds.
3. "I know that, but I am wondering how I shall get the paint off after-wards."	3. The man said that he knew that, but he was wondering how he would get the paint off afterwards.

Indirect	*Direct*
1. He said that he wanted me to spend a year in Paris and a year in Germany so that I could get a really good knowledge of French and German.	1. Pedro's father said: "I want you to spend a year in Paris and a year in Germany so that you can get a really good knowledge of French and German."
2. He said that my picture would hang in the British Museum long after Rubens and Rembrandt were forgotten.	2. He said: "Your picture will hang in the British Museum long after Rubens and Rembrandt are forgotten."
3. He said that in nine or ten years' time he wanted to retire, and by that time I should be able to run the business.	3. He said: "In nine or ten years' time I want to retire, and by that time you will be able to run the business."

You will notice that in reported speech the verbs that were in the *Present* Tense in direct speech become *Past* Tense in reported speech.

The only life *is* a life of art	becomes	The only life *was* a life of art
You *can* get a good knowledge of English	becomes	I *could* get a good knowledge of English
Your picture *will* hang	becomes	My picture *would* hang

I *want* to retire } becomes { He *wanted* to retire

It is natural that we should use the Past Tense, because we are reporting something that was said in the past.

The Past Tense of *will* is *would*, and the Past Tense of *shall* is *should*. At first sight it may seem rather a contradiction to speak of putting *shall* and *will*, which, as you know, are used to form the Future Tense, into a Past Tense. It is true that if Olaf says "I know it will be pleasant in England", he is referring to a future time and so he uses the Future Tense with *will*. But, when he says to Pedro: "I knew it would be pleasant in England", he is taking his mind back into the past and is speaking about what was, at that time, a future idea. So this usage of *should* and *would* is called **Future in the Past.**

I have said that the Past Tense (i.e. "future in the past") of *will* is *would* and of *shall* is *should*. Examples like the following seem to contradict this rule:

Direct	Indirect
"I am wondering how I *shall* get the paint off."	He was wondering how he *would* get the paint off.
"You *will* be able to run the business."	He said that I *should* be able to run the business.

But the use of *would* and *should* is the same as the

use of *shall* and *will*. You remember the forms of *shall* and *will*:

I shall We shall
You will They will
He, she, it will

The usage with *should* and *would* is:

I should We should
You would You would
He, she, it would They would

So, in the examples just given, *I shall* (1st Person) becomes *he would* (3rd Person); *you will* (2nd Person) becomes *I should* (1st Person).

You will notice, too, that when you turn Direct Speech into Reported Speech, the pronouns and pronoun adjectives (e.g. *my*, *his*, *your*) are also changed, e.g.

Direct	*Indirect*
Pedro said: "*I* want to go to Cambridge."	Pedro said that *he* wanted to go to Cambridge.
Olaf said: "*I* am going into *my* father's office."	Olaf said that *he* was going into *his* father's office.
The firm said: "*We* have removed *your* picture of the gas-works."	The firm said that *they* had removed *his* picture of the gas-works.

And one more point: quotation marks (" ") are not used in writing down Indirect Speech.

EXERCISES

I. *Give the exact words of the speaker in the following sentences, i.e. turn them from Indirect Speech into Direct Speech. Don't forget the quotation marks.*

1. Olaf said that he was staying in England for another year.
2. Hob said that his friend was a painter.
3. My father said that I could go to England for a year or two.
4. Olaf said that his father did a lot of business with England.
5. Olaf said that he could run that part of the business.
6. Hob said that he knew a man who was a painter.
7. The painter said that he wanted to paint the old man.
8. The painter said that he would pay him two pounds.
9. The teacher said that Olaf would never paint well.
10. Hiram Boost said that he knew the English Government wouldn't let him take the picture out of England.

11. Hob said his first impressions of England were connected with food.
12. Lucille said he didn't need to tell them that.
13. Pedro said that he wanted to go to Cambridge.
14. John said that he was up at Oxford.
15. Hob said that he would do the exercises later.
16. Mr. Priestley said that he would be surprised if they were done at all.
17. Mr. Wiggins said that he would never take Grandma out for a picnic again.
18. Jan said he had enjoyed his holiday in Switzerland.
19. Frieda said that he must come again.
20. Mr. Wiggins said that he was going to paint the sitting-room.
21. Timothy said that he wanted to help.
22. Hob said that that exercise had a lot of sentences.
23. Olaf said that there were only thirty.
24. Hob said that he called thirty a lot.
25. Olaf said that he could do them in a quarter of an hour.
26. The schoolmaster said that I should be able to win the race easily.
27. I said that I would try my best.
28. Lucille said she was going to drive her friend's car.
29. Hob said that none of his friends had a car.
30. Olaf said he enjoyed travelling by train.

II. *Turn the following sentences into Indirect Speech:*

1. Hob said, "My friend is a painter."
2. Olaf said, "I am staying in England for another year."
3. My father said, "You can go to England for a year or two."
4. Olaf said, "When you get to know the work of a shipping office it is most interesting."
5. OLAF: "My father does a lot of business with England."
6. OLAF: "Nothing will make me go into an office."
7. HOB: "I know a man who is a painter."
8. The firm said, "We have removed the picture of London gas-works."

9. OLAF: "I don't think office work will be interesting."
10. The painter said, "I will pay you two pounds."
11. Hob said, "I want more breakfast."
12. The waiter said to Hob, "I will fetch some for you."
13. Hob said, "I have never eaten a bigger meal in my life."
14. Mrs. Priestley said, "I must go to the butcher's."
15. She said to Lilian, "You can come with me."
16. Lilian said, "I will go and fetch your basket."
17. Mr. Priestley said, "Sally needs some more fish."
18. OLAF: "There is no life like a painter's."
19. HOB: "I am good at painting."
20. Olaf said to him, "I never knew that you could paint."
21. HOB: "I paint only doors and walls and windows."
22. LUCILLE: "I want to go to Germany, so that I can get a really good knowledge of German."
23. FRIEDA: "My sister and I spent six months in Frankfurt, and we enjoyed it very much."
24. She added, "I will go back there some day, if I ever have enough money."
25. OLAF: "A knowledge of German is very useful in my father's business."
26. MR. PRIESTLEY TO HIS STUDENTS: "I am going to give you an exercise on Indirect Speech. It will not be easy, but if you are thoughtful you can do it, as I have given you all the information that you need. You can look in your book if you wish, but I don't want you to ask anyone to help you."

III. *Choose the correct verb from the words in brackets:*

1. I said that I didn't (understand, understood) this sentence.
2. The porter knew that the train (would, will, had) be late.
3. The waiter said that there (was, is, had, are) no more bacon.
4. He said that I (should, can, could) be able to get some later.
5. Mr. Priestley told me that I was (speak, speaking, spoken) very well.

6. He added that it was hard to tell I (was, has, am) not an Englishman.
7. I said that he had (teach, taught, learned) me very well.
8. Pedro said that a man who (dressed, clothed, dresses) well, always got on well in business.
9. Mr. Priestley said that it always rained when he (forgets, forgot, forgotten) his umbrella.
10. Hob said he (knows, knew, had known) a funny story about that.

LESSON 4

Olaf Reads Another of His Plays

OLAF: I have written another little play about those funny neighbours of mine, the Wiggins family. May I read it to you?

MR. PRIESTLEY: Please do, Olaf. I am sure we shall all enjoy it.

OLAF: Here it is.

MR. WIGGINS PAINTS THE SITTING-ROOM

SCENE: *The sitting-room of the Wiggins' home.* GRANDMA *and* GRANDPA *are seated by the fire. Enter* MRS. WIGGINS *with a paint-brush,* TIMOTHY *with a pot of paint, and last* MR. WIGGINS *having some trouble with a large ladder.*

GRANDMA: It certainly is time this room was painted, isn't it, Grandpa?

GRANDPA: Indeed it is. I hope the job's going to be done properly. As I always say, if a job's worth doing, it's—er—er. What is it I always say, Grandma?

GRANDMA: If a job's worth doing, it's worth doing properly.

GRANDPA: Ah, yes, that's it. You know, James, if it wasn't for my rheumatism I'd paint the room myself.

MRS. WIGGINS: That's very kind of you, Grandpa, but James will manage; I'll see to that. You know, this is going to brighten up the room for you a lot. James, get up the ladder, and I'll pass the paint up.

TIMOTHY: Oh, look! Daddy nearly fell off!

MRS. WIGGINS: Well, hold the ladder, then, Timothy. We don't want your father to fall; paint makes a terrible mess on the floor. Now here's the paint, James. Be careful with it.

GRANDPA: Ah, you've forgotten something already. You haven't stirred the paint.

MRS. WIGGINS: I do think you might have remembered that, James. Pass it down again.

GRANDMA: Grandpa never used to forget a simple thing like that.

MRS. WIGGINS: Now, here's the paint, James. Come on, make a start.

MR. WIGGINS: You haven't handed me the brush yet.

MRS. WIGGINS: Timothy, hand your father the brush.

(Timothy lets go of the ladder and passes up the brush)

MR. WIGGINS: Here, hold the ladder. I nearly fell.

MRS. WIGGINS: That was your fault, Timothy.

TIMOTHY: Well, I can't do two things at once.

GRANDMA: You'd better be careful, James. You might get hurt badly if you fell off that ladder.

GRANDPA: A man who helped in my grocer's shop, broke his back falling from that height. He never left his bed again, poor fellow.

MR. WIGGINS: Well, here goes! How's that?

GRANDMA: Oh, what a terrible colour! Surely you're not going to paint the room green. It makes me feel quite ill.

MRS. WIGGINS: I know just what you need, Grandma. Timothy, go and put the kettle on, and we'll make Grandma a nice cup of tea.

(Timothy lets go of the ladder and goes into the kitchen)

GRANDPA: You're not holding the brush right, James. You won't get a smooth surface like that.

GRANDMA: You always got a beautiful finish, Grandpa.

MR. WIGGINS: Here, who's holding the ladder? It's not safe.

MRS. WIGGINS. Don't make such a fuss, James. Timothy is just getting some tea for poor Grandma. I'll hold the ladder.

GRANDMA: You haven't done much yet, James. I don't know when you will finish at that rate.

GRANDPA: I expect it will be like painting the Forth Bridge. When they've finished at one end, they have to start again at the other, eh?

GRANDMA: At least they don't paint the Forth Bridge green.

MRS. WIGGINS: James, your brush is dripping.

GRANDMA: It's very difficult to clean paint marks off the floor. I've a friend who scrubbed for two hours at a spot of paint and couldn't get it off.

MRS. WIGGINS: You must be more careful, James. Did you hear what Grandma said?

MR. WIGGINS (*a strange note in his voice*): Yes, I've heard all right what everybody's said.

GRANDMA: Of course, Grandpa was always a very clean painter. He used to paint our grocer's shop from top to bottom, and there was never a spot to clean.

GRANDPA: The best-looking shop in town, it was.

GRANDMA: You used red and white for it, and very nice the shop looked. People never painted rooms green in my young days. Where's that cup of tea, Nellie? I need something to cheer me up with that horrible colour spreading all over the wall.

MRS. WIGGINS: Timothy, hasn't the kettle boiled yet?

TIMOTHY: Nearly.

MRS. WIGGINS: Well, I'll go and make the tea.

MR. WIGGINS: Nobody's holding this ladder. It's moving all over the place.

GRANDMA: You nearly came off that time, James.

MR. WIGGINS: Well, come and hold the ladder, then.

GRANDMA: Don't shout at us, James. We're not deaf.

GRANDPA: I suppose I'd better help him, though my rheumatism will be back for certain.

GRANDMA: Don't you do it, Grandpa. James will be all right if he takes a bit of care.

GRANDPA: No, I'll do it. I don't mind suffering in a good cause. I may be able to give James some useful advice.

MR. WIGGINS: I don't need advice, thank you. All I need is someone to hold the ladder.

MRS. WIGGINS (*returning with the tea*): Now, don't be ungrateful, James. It's very good of Grandpa to offer advice. Now, here's your cup of tea Grandma.

GRANDMA: I must say I *need* it, too.

MR. WIGGINS: Here, Timothy, take this picture, will you? It's getting in my way.

TIMOTHY: Isn't it a funny picture. That girl does look silly with all those old clothes on.

MRS. WIGGINS: Not so loud, Timothy. That's a picture of Grandma when she was young.

GRANDMA: What did the boy say about me?

MRS. WIGGINS: He just said it's interesting how fashions change, Grandma.

GRANDMA: Yes, indeed. No one would have painted a room green in my young days. And I must say James seems to need a lot of people standing round the bottom of the ladder helping. Grandpa always did the painting on his own.

GRANDPA: That's so. It's all a matter of knowing how to do the job. An army of helpers is quite unnecessary if you do the job properly.

MR. WIGGINS: Here, hold the ladder steady, Grandpa. It's slipping.

TIMOTHY: Look out! The paint-pot's falling!

MR. WIGGINS: Hold the ladder!

TIMOTHY: The paint's all over Grandpa.

MRS. WIGGINS: James, why didn't you take more care?

GRANDPA: Get this pot off my head!

GRANDMA: If only it hadn't been green!

TIMOTHY: Grandpa's not just a grocer any more.
He's a *green*grocer.

EXERCISES

I. *Use the following words and phrases in sentences:*

1. ladder	6. deaf	11. terrible	16. drip
2. stir	7. advice	12. brush	17. bottom
3. steady	8. scrub	13. hurt	18. suffer
4. smooth	9. fashion	14. fellow	19. cheer up
5. surface	10. manage	15. fuss	20. for certain

II. *Put in the missing prepositions:*

1. Here's the paint, be careful — it.
2. You might get hurt if you fell — that ladder; a man broke his back falling — that height.
3. Timothy lets go — the ladder and goes — the kitchen.
4. You will never finish it — that rate.
5. It will be like the painting — the Forth Bridge. When they've finished at one end they have to start again — the other.
6. I've a friend who scrubbed — two hours — a spot — paint.
7. He used to paint our grocer's shop — top — bottom.
8. I need something to cheer me up — that horrible colour spreading all — the wall.
9. What did the boy say — me?

10. Grandpa always did the painting — his own.
11. Don't worry. I'll see — that.
12. Grandma was seated — the fire.
13. Mr. Wiggins had some trouble — the ladder.
14. He climbed — the ladder till he reached the top.
15. Don't shout — us.

III. *Put in question phrases:*

1. It's time this room was painted, — —?
2. You could paint very well, — —?
3. That was Timothy's fault, — —?
4. That wasn't Timothy's fault, — —?
5. You're not going to paint it that colour, — —?
6. Your brush is dripping, — —?
7. Your brush isn't dripping, — —?
8. You haven't done much, — —?
9. Daddy nearly fell off, — —?
10. Your father didn't fall off, — —?

IV. *Express in one word the meaning of each of the following phrases.* All the answers are words used in this lesson. You are given the first letter of each word and the number of letters in it.

1. To move something round with a stick or spoon. (s – – –)
2. To make more cheerful and full of colour. (b – – – – – – –)
3. Mistake; something for which you can be blamed. (f – – – –)
4. A piece of work. (j – –)
5. To succeed in doing something. (m – – – – –)
6. In the correct way. (p – – – – – – –)
7. To rub hard with a brush. (s – – – –)
8. Used to boil water in. (k – – – – –)
9. The lowest part of something. (b – – – – –)
10. Without any rough parts. (s – – – – –)

Composition Exercises

1. Tell or write the story of "Mr. Wiggins Paints the Sitting-room".

2. Tell or write any experiences you have had of painting—whether it was the painting of a wall, a door, or a picture;

or

Describe your favourite picture.

LESSON 5

Direct and Indirect Speech (ii)

QUESTIONS AND COMMANDS

A Simple sentence can do three things: (1) make a statement; (2) ask a question; (3) express a command or a request. We have seen how direct statements can be turned into indirect statements, so now let us see how direct **questions** and **commands** are expressed in the indirect form.

Indirect Questions

Notice what happens when we put a direct question into the indirect form.

Direct Question	*Indirect Question*
Pedro: "How much longer are you staying in England, Olaf?"	Pedro asked how much longer Olaf was staying in England.
The old fisherman: "How much will the artist pay me?"	The old fisherman asked how much the artist would pay him.
The picture firm to Mr. Boost: "When do you want us to stop?"	The picture firm asked Mr. Boost when he wanted them to stop.

Direct Question	Indirect Question
Grandpa: "What is it I always say, Grandma?"	Grandpa asked Grandma what it was he always said.
Grandma: "Where's that cup of tea, Nellie?"	Grandma asked where the cup of tea was.

Now there are three things to notice here in addition to the change in the pronouns and in the tense of the verbs:

(1) In the indirect question we use a verb like *ask* instead of *say*.

(2) There is a change in word order. The "question" form of the verb (verb before the subject), that is used in a direct question, becomes the "statement" form (verb after the subject) in the indirect question.

"...are you staying?" becomes "he was staying."

"...will the artist pay?" becomes "...the artist would pay..."

"...when do you want?" becomes "...when he wanted..."

"...did you hear?" becomes "if he heard."

"...where is that cup?" becomes "...where that cup was..."

(3) In indirect questions, the question mark is omitted.

Let us have some further examples:

Direct Question	Indirect Question
Olaf to Lucille: "Where are you going for your holidays?"	Olaf asked Lucille where she was going for her holidays.
Andrew (to shopkeeper): "How much is that bicycle?"	Andrew asked how much that bicycle was.
Olaf said, "When will you get back from Paris, Pedro?"	Olaf asked Pedro when he would get back from Paris.
Olaf said, "How long does it take to get from Paris to London?"	Olaf asked Pedro how long it took to get from Paris to London.
Hob said, "Can you swim, Andrew?"	Hob asked Andrew if he could swim.
Jan (to Mr. Priestley): "Shall I finish my exercise at home?"	Jan asked Mr. Priestley if he should finish his exercise at home.
Hob: "May I have another piece of cake, please?"	Hob asked if he might have another piece of cake.
Lucille (to Frieda): "Do you like my new dress?"	Lucille asked Frieda if (whether) she liked her new dress.

Indirect Commands

Direct Command	Indirect Command
Macasso to Hob: "Go out and speak to the fisherman."	Macasso told Hob to go out and speak to the fisherman.
Art teacher to Olaf: "Go back to your office."	The art teacher told Olaf to go back to his office.
Olaf to Pedro and Hob: "Come and spend a holiday with me in Sweden."	Olaf asked (invited) Pedro and Hob to spend a holiday with him in Sweden.
Art teacher to Olaf: "Don't come for any more lessons."	The art teacher told Olaf not to come for any more lessons.

Notice: (1) An indirect command is introduced by a word like *told, ordered, commanded*.

(2) In direct commands we use the Imperative form of the verb; in indirect commands we don't use the Imperative, we use the Infinitive.

(3) A negative direct command begins: "Don't ..." (or "Do not ..."). When this is turned into an indirect command, "do" is omitted and *don't* becomes simply *not*.

Here are some further examples of direct and indirect commands:

Direct Command	Indirect Command
Andrew to his dog: "Lie down, Jock."	Andrew ordered Jock to lie down.
Officer to soldiers: "Fire!"	The officer commanded the soldiers to fire.
The teacher said to the boy, "Come in."	The teacher told the boy to come in.
Mr. Priestley said to Hob: "Write your work more carefully or I shan't read it."	Mr. Priestley told Hob to write his work more carefully or he wouldn't read it.

INDIRECT STATEMENTS ARE INTRODUCED BY "SAID", INDIRECT QUESTIONS BY "ASKED", INDIRECT COMMAND BY "TOLD", ETC.

Direct Command (negative)	Indirect Command (negative)
Teacher (to his class): "Don't waste your time."	The teacher told his class not to waste their time.
Andrew's father said: "Don't climb that tree in your new trousers."	Andrew's father told him not to climb that tree in his new trousers.

Sometimes the Imperative form of the verb expresses a request rather than a command. The construction for requests is the same as that for commands, but the indirect form is introduced by a word like *asked*, *requested*, etc., e.g.

Direct Request	Indirect Request
Mother (to Andrew): "Please don't eat all the cake."	Mother asked Andrew not to eat all the cake.
Farmer (to visitors): "Please don't leave the gate open."	The farmer asked (requested) the visitors not to leave the gate open.
Frieda (to Jan): "Pass me the sugar, please."	Frieda asked (requested) Jan to pass her the sugar.

* * * *

LESSON FIVE

FRIEDA: Thank you, Mr. Priestley; I have understood your explanation of direct and indirect speech; but there was one word that you used—I wrote it down—and I'm not quite sure of its meaning. It was "contradict".

MR. PRIESTLEY: Its general meaning is "to say the opposite"; "to declare that a thing just said is not true". So if Olaf said:

"The sun rises in the west"

Pedro might say: "I'm sorry to contradict you, Olaf, but the sun rises in the east." When I said "will" and "shall" are used to express an idea in the *future*, and then added, "the *past* form of 'will' is 'would' and of 'shall' is 'should'," that looked like a contradiction. Is the meaning quite clear now?

FRIEDA: Oh yes, thank you.

HOB: I think a drink that an Englishman has ought to be called "Contradiction".

PEDRO: Whatever do you mean?

HOB: Well, he wants a *strong* drink, so he chooses whiskey; then he adds water to make it *weak*. He puts in lemon to make it *sour*, and then adds sugar to make it *sweet*. He holds up his glass and says to his friend, "Here's to *you*"; and then he drinks it *himself*!

EXERCISES

I. *Give the exact words of the speaker in the following sentences (i.e. turn the sentences from indirect to direct speech). Don't forget quotation marks, and question marks where necessary.*

1. Mr. Priestley asked Hob how much longer he would take over the exercise.
2. Hob asked if it was lunch-time yet.
3. Margaret asked where Sally had gone.
4. Andrew said he had seen her in the garden.
5. Mrs. Priestley asked Olaf how his neighbour, Mr. Wiggins, was getting on.
6. Frieda asked how much Lucille's new skirt had cost.
7. Andrew asked Lilian if she was going out shopping.
8. Margaret asked if she could go for a swim.
9. Mrs. Priestley asked the butcher what the price of the beef was.
10. Olaf asked the station-master if he should catch the train from Victoria to get to Brighton.
11. Andrew asked if he might have some more chocolate.
12. Lilian told Andrew not to eat it all.
13. The teacher told the class to pay attention.
14. He told them not to go on talking.
15. The officer ordered the soldiers to stay in the woods.
16. Frieda invited Jan to come and spend a holiday in Switzerland.
17. Mr. Wiggins told Timothy to pass up the paint.
18. Grandma told Mr. Wiggins not to use that colour.
19. Mr. Wiggins asked Olaf if he liked the colour.
20. Olaf said that he thought it was very nice.

II. *Rewrite these sentences in indirect speech:*

1. ANDREW: "How much is that dog in the window?"
2. PEDRO: "When are you leaving England, Olaf?"

3. LUCILLE: "How shall I get to the dance in time?"
4. MR. PRIESTLEY TO HOB: "Can you do the exercise on Indirect Questions?"
5. HOB: "Shall I try it?"
6. OLAF TO JAN: "Come for a bicycle ride with me next week-end."
7. MRS. PRIESTLEY TO THE JEWELLER: "When will my watch be repaired?"
8. MRS. WIGGINS: "Don't make such a fuss, James."
9. GRANDPA: "You're not holding the brush right, James."
10. The teacher said to the class, "You must work harder."
11. Mr. Priestley said to me, "Have you ever been to Venice?"
12. MRS. WIGGINS: "Did you hear what Grandpa said, James?"
13. Andrew said to Jock: "Don't go away."
14. THE OFFICER TO THE SOLDIERS: "Fire at the enemy!"
15. Mrs. Priestley said to Margaret, "Take more care of your clothes or I shan't have time to repair them before we go on our holiday."

16. *Here is a short story containing Direct Statements, Questions and Commands. Rewrite it in Indirect Speech. Begin "The writer said that . . ." (Call the ant "he" and the grasshopper "she".)*

The Ant and the Grasshopper

I will tell you the story of the ant and the grasshopper. It is a cold winter's day and an ant is bringing out some grains of corn that he had gathered in the summer as he wants to dry them. A grasshopper, who is very hungry, sees him and says, "Give me a few grains of corn; I am dying of hunger."

"But," says the ant, "what did you do in the summer? Didn't you store up some corn?"

"No," replies the grasshopper, "I was too busy."

"What did you do?" says the ant.

"I sang all day," answers the grasshopper.

"If you sang all summer," says the ant, "you can dance all winter."

III. *Contradict these wrong statements, beginning "I'm sorry to contradict you but . . ."*

1. There are eleven pennies in a shilling.
2. Glasgow is the capital of Scotland.
3. The sun moves round the earth.
4. It costs seven pence to send a letter from London to Paris.
5. Hob gets all his exercises right.

LESSON 6

Mrs. Priestley Tells a Story and Mr. Priestley Puts Up a Hen-house

[Do you remember Andrew Macaulay, Mr. Priestley's nephew ? We met him in Book II (Lesson 10). He is staying again at the Priestleys' for a short holiday, so we'll look into the sitting-room and listen to their talk. Andrew is about eleven years old.]

ANDREW : I wish I had a million pounds.

MARGARET PRIESTLEY : Why, Andrew ?

ANDREW : I'd buy a motor-boat, a big car like Lucille's, and I'd go all over the world. I'd be the happiest boy alive.

MARGARET : I don't think you would.

ANDREW : Of course I should. With all that money I could have everything I wanted. Don't you think so, Uncle Charles ?

MR. PRIESTLEY : I don't know, Andrew ; I've never had a million pounds, and I'm not sure that I should recognise a happy man if I saw one.

ANDREW : Aunt Mary, you agree with me don't you ?

MRS. PRIESTLEY : Well, I don't know, but that last remark of your Uncle Charles reminds me of an old story . . . but you've probably heard it.

ANDREW and MARGARET : Oh no, I'm sure I haven't. Please tell us a story.

MRS. PRIESTLEY : Well, I'll tell you the story—but after that it's bedtime for both of you.

43

Once upon a time (all old stories begin like that), and in a country a long way off, there was a king who was very ill. All the doctors of the court attended him but, in spite of all they could do, he got worse instead of better. At last in despair they called in a famous doctor from another country. He came, looked at the king, and then, looking very grave, said, "Your Majesty, there is only one thing that can cure you."

"What is that ?" said the king. "Whatever you want shall be brought for you."

"You must sleep for one night," said the doctor, "in the shirt of a happy man!"

So the king sent two of his chief servants to find a happy man and, when they had found him, to bring back his shirt.

Well, they went first to the richest man in the city, and asked him if he was a happy man.

"Happy!" he said, "when I never know whether my ships are going to be wrecked next day, when thieves are always trying to break into my house. How can a man be happy with all these worries ?"

So they went to the king's Chief Minister, the most powerful man in the country, except for the king.

"Are you a happy man ?" they said.

"Don't be silly," he said. "There's Ruritania threatening to make war on us any day. There's that villain Popoff trying to push me out of power, the workers are always wanting to have more money, and the wealthy wanting to pay less taxes. How do you think a Chief Minister can be a happy man?"

So they went all over the country looking high and low for a happy man but never finding one.

They were returning home, tired and miserable (for they quite expected that the king would have them put to death for not finding what he wanted), when they saw a beggar, sitting by the roadside. He had made a little fire, and was frying some sausages in a frying-pan, and singing merrily as he watched his supper cooking.

They looked at each other. Had they found what they were looking for? They went up to him and one of them said, "You sound very happy, my friend."

"Of course, I'm happy," he said.

They could hardly believe their ears. With one voice they said, "We want your shirt."

The beggar roared with laughter.

"I'm sorry, gentlemen," he said, "but I haven't got a shirt."

MARGARET: Oh, Mummy, what a nice story. You are nearly as good as Hob at telling stories.

MRS. PRIESTLEY: Thank you, dear. And now come on, bedtime!

MR. PRIESTLEY: Yes, Andrew, get to bed early, I've a big job for you and me in the morning.

ANDREW: Oh, Uncle Charles, what is it?

MR. PRIESTLEY: You'll hear tomorrow morning. Good night.

* * * *

The Next Morning

ANDREW and MR. PRIESTLEY

ANDREW: What's the job, Uncle Charles, that you want me to help you with?

MR. PRIESTLEY: Well, we are getting ten new hens and I want a house for them. I've bought a hen-house, it arrived yesterday afternoon, but it's in parts and needs to be put together.

ANDREW: That's just the sort of job I like.

MR. PRIESTLEY: Come on then to the back-garden.

*　　　*　　　*　　　*

(Between you and me, I don't feel too hopeful about the success of this job. Mr. Priestley is all right at teaching English, but I shouldn't call him a good "practical" man. And as for Andrew, well, he has all the confidence of a boy of eleven. We'll leave it at that and go to the back-garden and watch them.)

*　　　*　　　*　　　*

The Back-garden

MR. PRIESTLEY: Right. Now let's get to work. Here are the parts. These two long ones will be the sides, I think. That one will be the back and that one the front.

ANDREW: Oh yes, and the other piece will be the roof. It's easy. We'll soon have it up.

MR. PRIESTLEY: Well, it may not be so easy as it looks, but we'll try what we can do.

ANDREW: Have you all the tools: hammer, nails, saw, screws, screwdriver?

MR. PRIESTLEY: Here are nails and a hammer. We shan't need a saw; the wood is sawn into the right sizes already. And I don't think we'll need screws or screwdriver.

ANDREW: Suppose we put the back and one side into position and I will hold them there while you nail them together.

MR. PRIESTLEY: I don't think we should nail them together. The makers of the hen-house have sent a small bag of nuts and bolts. We should bolt them together.

ANDREW: Oh yes, that's right. Look, there's a hole here for the bolt to go in. Now I'll hold the side and end together while you push the bolt through the hole. Oh! look out!

(There's a crash as the side falls down)

Sorry, Uncle Charles, the wind caught that side and I couldn't hold it. I hope it didn't hurt your foot.

MR. PRIESTLEY: Oh, it's nothing much; I'm probably lamed for life, but never mind. I think, Andrew, it would be better if *I* held the side and you pushed the bolt through the hole.

ANDREW: Right ho! Here it comes.—You see it?

MR. PRIESTLEY: Yes. That's all right. Now you come to this side, put the nut on and screw it up tight with the spanner. . . . Good. Now we'll put on the other side in the same way. Push the bolt through the holes, put the nut on and screw it up.

ANDREW: We are getting on well, aren't we, Uncle Charles; we can put the front on now. I'll go inside and push the bolt through and you can screw the nut on.

... It doesn't seem to go through very well.

(That's probably because they are putting it through from the wrong side; the nut ought to be on the inside!)

I'll get a hammer and knock it through.

MR. PRIESTLEY: All right, but be careful what you do.

ANDREW:.Oh, I know how to use a hammer. (*Knock*) ... It's going ... (*Knock*) ... (CRASH!)

MR. PRIESTLEY: Now what's happened?

ANDREW: Oh, I'm sorry, Uncle Charles; the hammer slipped out of my hand and went through the window. I'm afraid the glass is no use now.

MR. PRIESTLEY: Oh, well, it's no use crying over spilt milk. I'll go to the shop tomorrow and ask them to cut me another piece of glass.

ANDREW: We'll put the roof on now. I'll stay inside and see that it fits properly. You just nail it on, don't you; I don't see any holes for bolts. Here's the hammer and you've plenty of nails outside You should drive some nails in here . . . (*Knock, knock*) . . . Good! . . . now some more nails all round here (*Knock, knock, knock*).—That's very good . . . just one or two more and the roof will be on (*Knock, knock, knock*). Oh, splendid, that's the job done. I'll come out now and see what it looks like from outside. . . .

Hey! I say, how do I get out? The door's locked.

MR. PRIESTLEY: Well, unlock it; isn't the key inside?

ANDREW: No; isn't it outside?

MR. PRIESTLEY: No; the makers must have forgotten to send me a key!

*　　　*　　　*　　　*

(I think at this point we'd better go away and leave them to it.)

EXERCISES

I. *Use the following words and phrases in sentences:*

1. million	6. threaten	11. fry
2. attend	7. villain	12. merrily
3. in spite of	8. tax	13. practical
4. grave (adj.)	9. minister	14. confidence
5. wreck	10. beggar	15. leave it at that

16. tools	21. screwdriver
17. saw (noun)	22. lame
18. saw (verb)	23. spanner
19. screw	24. never mind
20. nuts and bolts	25. remark (noun)

II. *Explain the meaning of the following:*

1. It's no use crying over spilt milk.
2. We are getting on well.
3. They could hardly believe their ears.
4. Between you and me.
5. Right ho!

III. *Put in the missing words, so that the sentences make sense:*

1. I wish I — a million pounds.
2. I don't think that I — recognise a happy man — if I saw one.
3. You — reminded me of a story, but I expect you have — it before.
4. Once — — — there was a king — was ill.
5. The — suggestion for curing the king was a — one.
6. There is — one thing that can — you.
7. The king sent servants to find the — of a man — was happy.
8. They had no — . Nobody seemed to be — .
9. As they — home they noticed a beggar — by the roadside.
10. He was — sausages over a little — , and he — merrily as his supper was — .
11. They thought that at last they had — what they were looking — .
12. They were wrong. The beggar — no shirt.
13. Andrew was full of — , and Mr. Priestley was better at — English — putting up a hen-house.
14. That's just the — of job I like.
15. Now let's — to work.

IV. *Give questions to which the following are answers.*
You will find these openings helpful: "Where?"
"How much?" "Did you?" "What?" "Why?"
"Have you?" "How old?" "When?" "How
many?"

1. I'd buy a motor-boat and a big car.
2. No, I've never heard a story about a happy man's shirt before.
3. It's just five to four.
4. Because ten new hens are coming tomorrow.
5. The 3½ pence stamp is green.
6. He is eleven years old.
7. I am going to North Wales this year.
8. No, I looked up, but it had flown away.
9. I first came to England in 1955.
10. The hen-house cost £5.22½p.
11. He was singing and frying sausages.
12. He said there was only one thing that could cure him.
13. Mr. Priestley had ordered ten new hens.
14. No, he didn't succeed in unlocking the door.
15. Because the makers had forgotten to send a key.

V. *Explain the use of:*

1. A hammer. 2. A nail. 3. A screwdriver. 4. A lock on a door. 5. A frying-pan. 6. A saw.

Composition Exercises

Tell or write the story of:

(a) The Happy Man's Shirt.
(b) Mr. Priestley, Andrew and the hen-house.
(c) Say or write what you would do if you had a million pounds.

LESSON 7

Sentences and Clauses

Let us start with a few definitions; first of all the definition of a **sentence.**

A sentence is a group of words that makes complete sense. It generally does one of three things: (1) it makes a statement; (2) it asks a question; (3) it gives a command or makes a request, e.g.

> I am teaching you English.   (*Statement*)
> Do you understand that?   (*Question*)
> Bring your book here.   (*Command*)
> Please help me with my work. (*Request*)

Each of these sentences has only one finite verb in it; so each is a **Simple Sentence.**

Two or more sentences may be joined together by a conjunction (or conjunctions), e.g.

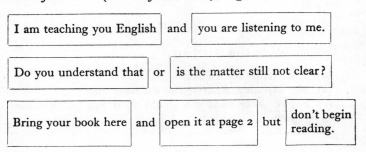

52

Two or more simple sentences joined by conjunctions form a **Compound Sentence.**

Each of the sentences in a compound sentence makes complete sense by itself, and the sentences in a Compound Sentence are all of the same importance.

But there are some sentences that don't make complete sense by themselves. They contain a finite verb (as all sentences do), but they make sense only when they are used with another sentence. Here are some examples of sentences that don't make complete sense by themselves:

which I want; that he was tired; when he saw the policeman.

But if I put another sentence with each of them, then they do make sense, e.g.

That is the book *which I want.*
Hob said *that he was tired.*
The thief ran away *when he saw the policeman.*

Sentences which cannot stand alone are called **Clauses.** The sentences that support them are called

CLAUSES CANNOT STAND ALONE

Principal Clauses; the others are called **Subordinate** Clauses. A sentence that has one principal clause and one or more subordinate clauses is called a **Complex** sentence.

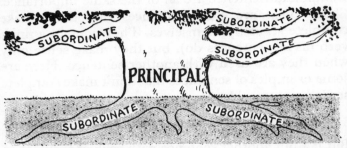

A COMPLEX SENTENCE CONTAINS ONE PRINCIPAL AND ONE OR MORE
SUBORDINATE CLAUSES

Principal Clause	Subordinate Clause
That is the book	which I want.
Hob said	that he was tired.
The thief ran away	when he saw the policeman.

Now let us look at the work that those three subordinate clauses are doing. The first tells us more about the noun *book*. It is doing the work of an adjective; it is **an Adjective Clause.**

The second is the object of the verb *said*. It is doing the work of a noun; it is a **Noun Clause.**

The third is doing the work of an adverb. It tells

us *when* the thief ran away. It is an **Adverb Clause.**
Those are the three kinds of subordinate clauses.

The subordinate clauses are joined to the principal
clauses by conjunctions, *which, that, when,* etc. But
which is rather more than a conjunction. Besides
joining sentences it also stands instead of a
noun; in our example it stands instead of the noun
book.

Let us look at some more examples of Adjective
Clauses:

1. That is the book *which I want.*
2. Here is Joe Marsden *who looks after Lucille's car.*
3. This is the house *that Jack built.*
4. That is the man *whom I met.*

These sentences could be written like this (though
they wouldn't then be very good):

1. That is the book *and* I want *it* (the book).
2. Here is Joe Marsden *and he* (Joe) looks after Lucille's car.
3. This is the house *and* Jack built *it* (the house).
4. That is the man *and* I met *him.*

You can see from this that the words *who, that,
which, whom* are doing the work of the conjunction
and, and are also doing the work of a pronoun, i.e.
standing instead of a noun. The words *who, which,
that* and *whom,* when they are used like this, are
called **Relative[1] Pronouns.** The noun for which the
relative pronoun stands (*book, Joe Marsden, house,
man*) is called the **Antecedent.[2]**

[1] Because they "relate", i.e. join, sentences together.
[2] "Antecedent" means "going before".

Let us put all this down in a form that will make it easy to understand.

PRINCIPAL CLAUSE		ADJECTIVE CLAUSE		*Work done by the adjective clause*
	Antecedent	*Relative Pronoun*		
That is	the book	which	I want	qualifies *book*
Here is	Joe Marsden	who	looks after Lucille's car	qualifies *Joe Marsden*
That is	the house	that	Jack built	qualifies *house*
There is	the man	whom	I met	qualifies *man*

The relative pronouns *who* and *whom* are used for people; *which* is used for things; *that* is for people and things. *Who* is the nominative form, *whom* is the objective form; *that* and *which* can be nominative or objective.

Sometimes the principal clause is divided into two by the adjective clause, like this:

1. The house ⎢ that Jack built ⎢ has fallen down.

2. Joe Marsden ⎢ who looks after Lucille's car ⎢ is a very good mechanic.

3. The book ⎢ which I want ⎢ is on the table.

4. The man | whom I met | knows Lucille.

If these sentences are not written in this form, they would not, in every case, express the meaning we want them to express, e.g.

> The book is on the table which I want.
> The man knows Lucille whom I met.

do not mean the same as:

> The book which I want is on the table.
> The man whom I met knows Lucille.

The general rule is:

Put the relative pronoun as near as possible to its antecedent.

Quite often, and especially in conversation, we leave out the relative pronoun if it is in the objective case. For example, the sentences:

> That is the girl $\begin{cases} \text{whom} \\ \text{that} \end{cases}$ I met at the party.
>
> Where is the boy $\begin{cases} \text{whom} \\ \text{that} \end{cases}$ you spoke to?
>
> The boy $\begin{cases} \text{whom} \\ \text{that} \end{cases}$ I spoke to was Andrew.
>
> The book $\begin{cases} \text{which} \\ \text{that} \end{cases}$ I want is on my study table.

can be written:

> That is the girl I met at the party.
> Where is the boy you spoke to?
> The boy I spoke to was Andrew.
> The book I want is on my study table.

You have seen that the relative pronoun *who* has an objective form *whom*. (It is the only relative pronoun that has more than one form.) *Who* has also a possessive form *whose*, e.g.

> That is the boy *whose* brother was killed.
> The girls, *whose* singing you admired, are in my class.
> He is a man *whose* name is known all over the world.

The word *as* is also a relative pronoun if it is used after *such* or *same*. Look at this sentence:

> Meet me at the place that you did yesterday.

Quite clearly *that* is a relative pronoun. But if you put the word *same* in the principal clause, then we use *as* instead of *that*, e.g.

> Meet me at the *same* place *as* you did yesterday.

So compare these sentences:

> 1. I never say the things *that* you say.
> 2. I never say *such* things *as* you say.

Here also, after the word *such*, *as* is a relative pronoun.

EXERCISES

I. *Say or write whether the following sentences are Simple, Compound or Complex:*

1. I like eggs and bacon.
2. Hob likes eggs and he often has three for breakfast.
3. I prefer eggs which are new-laid.
4. When Margaret is laughing and singing, we know she is happy.
5. Andrew wants to play with Sally, but Sally runs away.

II. *In the following sentences pick out the Adjective Clause. Write which word is the relative pronoun (if any), and which word is the antecedent.*

1. This is the hammer that Mr. Priestley used.
2. The window which Andrew hit is broken.
3. I enjoyed the book about the climbing of Everest, which you gave me for my birthday.
4. I met his brother, who teaches at a boarding-school.
5. The birds which flew away in the autumn have returned.
6. The boarding-school to which Andrew was sent is excellent.
7. Do you know the man whose house we have just passed?
8. Jock walked round the house in which Sally lived.
9. The dress Lucille is wearing suits her very well.
10. The train by which we travelled from Newhaven was very slow.
11. Frieda and Jan have just returned from a Bach concert, which was conducted by Sir Malcolm Sargent.
12. The composer I like best is Beethoven.
13. I hope to marry a girl who is a good cook.
14. The person who said the last sentence is Hob.
15. The landlady, whose rooms I had taken, took my luggage upstairs.

III. *Join each of these pairs of Simple Sentences into a Complex one by using relative pronouns (who, whom, which, that, whose). Don't use "that" in sentences marked *.*

1. I liked the story.   Hob told it.
2. *Here is the girl.   You spoke to her this morning.
3. I have read the book.   You told me about it.
4. There is the plane.   I came to London by it.
5. There is the man.   His dog bit me.
6. The plane has flown 10,000 miles.   I came to London in it.

7. Andrew's dog ran after a car. The dog is called Jock.
8. The bicycle was for my birthday. My Uncle Albert sent it.
9. That is the house. We lived in it in 1950.
10.*We liked the boy. You brought him to the house.
11. Our friend wrote a well-known book. He lives in that house.
12. I never saw such bad work. Hob has done it.
13. The apples grew on my tree. You are eating them.
14. The girl is going to sing a song. She is called Margaret.
15.*There is the boy. You saw him this morning.
16. Mary has invited us to tea. Her mother makes lovely cakes.
17. That is the same story. Hob told it.
18.*His brother is the headmaster of a school. I once met him in Beirut.
19. This man works at a garage. His name is Joe Marsden.
20. Joe Marsden works at a garage. He looks after Lucille's car.

LESSON 8

Adverb Clauses

MR. PRIESTLEY: I explained something about Adjective Clauses in Lesson 7, now I want to look a little more closely at Adverb Clauses.

An adverb of manner usually tells **how** an action was done; an adverb of time tells **when** it was done; an adverb of place tells **where** it was done, e.g.

Jan did his work *well*. (Manner)
I saw him *yesterday*. (Time)
We met the boys *there*. (Place)

Now Adverb Clauses do exactly the same work, e.g.

Jan did his work *as work ought to be done*. (Manner)
I saw him *when I was walking to the football field*. (Time)
We met the boys *where we generally meet them*. (Place)

But there are other kinds of Adverb Clauses besides Clauses of Manner, Time and Place. They all tell us something about the verb in the other sentence. And what they tell us enables us to decide what kind of Adverb Clauses they are. Some clauses express *why* something was done. They are Adverb Clauses of **Reason,** e.g.

The thief ran away *because he saw the policeman*.
Jan passed his examination *because he worked hard*.
Because he hadn't worked hard, Hob didn't pass his examination.

61

Some adverbial clauses tell us on what condition a thing will happen. These are Adverb Clauses of **Condition,** e.g.

> Olaf will pass his examination *if he works hard.*
> *If the rain stops,* I shall go for a walk.
> We will help you, *if you need help.*
> I cannot drink coffee *unless*[1] *it is well made.*

There is one other kind of Adverb Clause that, I think, you ought to know, the kind that expresses the purpose for doing something. These are called Adverb Clauses of **Purpose,** e.g.

> Olaf is working hard *so that he will pass his examination.*
> The thief hid behind the tree *so that the policeman would not see him.*
> Hob ate a big lunch before he went to London *so that he wouldn't be hungry on the way.*

ADVERB CLAUSES

Noun Clauses

You will often see a clause that is the object, or, much more rarely, the subject of a verb. The subjects

[1] *unless* it is = *if* it is *not*

or objects of verbs are usually nouns. So these clauses, which are doing the work of nouns are **Noun Clauses.** Here, for example, are some sentences where the object is a noun:

	OBJECT
I know Hob said George dreamed	*arithmetic.* a few *words.* a *dream.*

Now, instead of using nouns for objects of these verbs, we'll use a clause.

	OBJECT
I know Hob said George dreamed	*that two and two make four.* *that he would tell us a story.* *that he was flying to the moon.*

These are noun clauses.

Here are some sentences where the subject of the verb is a noun:

SUBJECT	
Your *work*	seems very difficult.
The prisoner's *escape*	is a complete mystery.

Once again, instead of using a noun we'll use a clause:

SUBJECT	
What you are doing	seems very difficult.
How the prisoner escaped	is a complete mystery.

There you have examples of Noun Clauses used as the subject of a sentence.

Analysis

For an exercise to test your knowledge of clauses and to see the construction of Complex sentences, you can analyse, that is break up, a Complex sentence like this:

Complex Sentence

When Mr. Priestley asked him a question, Olaf said that he knew the answer because it was in the lesson that he had just read.

Analysis

CLAUSE	KIND
When Mr. Priestley asked him a question	Adverb Clause of Time, qualifies "said"

CLAUSE	KIND
Olaf said	Principal
that he knew the answer	Noun Clause, object of "said"
because it was in the lesson	Adverb Clause of Reason, qualifies "knew"
that he had just read	Adjective Clause, qualifies "lesson"

Finally, here is a complex sentence containing a principal clause and three or four subordinate ones:

The boy, who was crying as if his heart would break, said, when I spoke to him, that he was hungry because he had had no food for two days.

Now I will analyse it into its separate clauses:

CLAUSE	KIND
The boy said	Principal Clause

CLAUSE	KIND
who was crying	Adjective Clause, describes "boy"
as if his heart would break	Adverb Clause (*Manner*)
when I spoke to him	Adverb Clause (*Time*)
that he was hungry	Noun Clause, object of "said"
because he had had no food for two days	Adverb Clause (*Reason*)

And that, I think, is all you need to know for the present about Complex Sentences.

EXERCISE

I. *Pick out the subordinate adverb clauses in the following sentences, and say or write what kind each one is (e.g. Manner, Condition, Purpose, etc.):*

1. Unless you drive home carefully, you will have an accident.
2. Andrew used the hammer, while Mr. Priestley held the side.
3. He went to the heart of Africa, so that he could shoot wild animals.
4. If the stamp is torn, it's no good for my collection.

5. Mr. Priestley wouldn't go to bed, until he had finished the last chapter of his new book.
6. Because the medicine tasted so unpleasant, Andrew usually forgot to drink it.
7. The policeman raised his hand so that the traffic would stop.
8. You will find it if you look carefully.
9. After it was dark, the battleship steamed into the bay.
10. The hammer lay where Andrew had dropped it.

II. Pick out the noun clauses in the following sentences:

1. Andrew said that he was taking Jock for a walk.
2. Hob hopes that Mr. Priestley won't ask him a question.
3. The pupil said that the questions were too difficult.
4. "They are quite easy," replied the teacher.
5. What you said was quite true.

III. Complete the following adverb clauses with suitable conjunctions, and say what sort of adverb clause it is:

1. — you have worked so hard, you may have a holiday.
2. You can't blame Mr. Priestley — Hob fails his exam.
3. I don't like coffee — it is really hot and strong.
4. — you are ready to go, I'll go with you.
5. Mrs. Priestley baked a cake — — the students would have something to eat at eleven o'clock.

IV. Analyse the following sentences:

1. Mr. Priestley, who is writing a new book, said that he did not hear the bell when the postman rang.
2. The thief, who had hidden the money under a tree, went back again because he thought that he could now take it away with safety.
3. When Mr. Priestley asked what part of speech a word was, Pedro said, "I can tell you the answer if you will give me a sentence in which the word is used."

LESSON 9

A Visit to Stratford

(*Lilian, Mr. Priestley's niece, is staying, with her brother Andrew, at the Priestleys' house. She writes a letter home.*)

April 24th.

Dear Mother and Father,

We had a heavenly day yesterday; Cousin John is home from Oxford for a short holiday (he calls it "vacation") so he took Margaret and Andrew and me in Uncle Charles's car to Stratford-on-Avon, the place where Shakespeare was born and died. It was a very suitable day, for yesterday was April 23rd; that is St. George's Day—the Saint of England—and that is the day on which Shakespeare was born,[1] and also the day on which he died.[2]

Stratford is a very interesting town, right in the centre of England. You can't get very far from the sea anywhere in England, but Stratford is about the farthest point you can get from it. It's nice to think that Shakespeare was born right in the heart of England and in the midst of country that is so typically English, quite unlike our Scottish[3] country

[1] 1564.   [2] 1616.   [3] Lilian's home is in Scotland.

round Inverness. There are no mountains or deep valleys near Stratford; there's nothing of the grand scenery that we have round the Cairngorms,[1] but there are beautiful woods, green fields, a quiet gentle river—the winding Avon—and lovely houses, black and white with thatched roofs.

Stratford is quite a busy town, especially on market day when the farmers from the countryside round Stratford come to buy or sell cows or pigs or sheep. At least so John told me, and he knows Stratford well. But it wasn't market day yesterday, so we were able to look round comfortably. The first place we went to was Shakespeare's birthplace, a small house with small rooms in the centre of Stratford. We saw the very room where Shakespeare was born. Lots of people who had visited the house had written their names on the walls. It seemed a wrong thing to do—although among the names were Walter Scott, Dickens, Thackeray and Browning.

In one room was a little wooden desk, the very desk that Shakespeare sat in when he went to the grammar school in Stratford. But one of the things I liked best was the garden behind the house, because in it are growing all the flowers, trees and plants that are mentioned in Shakespeare's plays.

When Shakespeare became successful in London he bought the biggest house in Stratford, a house called New Place, to retire to. Here he probably wrote *The Winter's Tale* and *The Tempest*; and here he died. Well, I wanted to see that; but there's nothing left of it but a few bricks and the garden. The man

---

[1] Mountains in the north of Scotland.

who owned it, Mr. Gastrell, was so bad-tempered, because so many people came to see the house, that he pulled it down.[1] It's hard to believe that, isn't it, but John said it's true. Shakespeare had planted a mulberry tree in the garden and Mr. Gastrell cut that down, too, but the people of Stratford took pieces of the tree and planted one of them in the garden of New Place, and that tree is still growing there. I'm sorry to say that while we were not looking at him, Andrew took a piece of it, about three inches long, from one of the branches. He said he knew Uncle Charles was very fond of Shakespeare and so he was going to plant his little piece in Uncle Charles's garden so that Uncle Charles could have a tree from "Shakespeare's tree".

Then we went to the church where Shakespeare is buried. There's a bust of Shakespeare that was carved by a Dutch sculptor who lived near Shakespeare's Globe Theatre and must have seen Shakespeare many a time, and on the stone of Shakespeare's grave are the lines

> Good friend, for Jesus' sake forbear
> To dig the dust enclosed here.
> Blest be the man that spares these stones
> And curst be he that moves my bones.

John said that, though it wasn't very good poetry, it was almost certainly written by Shakespeare himself. At any rate, I'm glad it has been successful in keeping anyone from "moving his bones".

By this time we were very hungry; Andrew had been saying for the last hour or so that he would be

[1] In 1758.

glad when it was time for lunch. So John took us to a very old hotel that was probably there in Shakespeare's time. It had some beautiful Tudor tables and chairs; and the rooms haven't numbers on the doors as most hotels have. Instead every room has the name of a Shakespeare play on it—the "Hamlet" room, the "Romeo and Juliet" room and so on. And we had a jolly good lunch there. After lunch John took us across the fields, about a mile out of Stratford, to Anne Hathaway's Cottage. Anne Hathaway was the woman that Shakespeare married, and the cottage is just as it was in Shakespeare's time. There are the old chairs by the fire-place where Shakespeare must have sat, the plates from which he probably ate his dinner, and a leather bottle from which Anne poured out beer for

SHAKESPEARE MEMORIAL THEATRE, STRATFORD

him. In that little house I felt as if I was living in the 17th century, and if Shakespeare had come walking down the narrow stairs I shouldn't have felt very surprised.

We had a look at the Shakespeare Memorial Theatre, built on rather plain practical lines (someone said it was "like a modern factory"), but John said it has the best stage in England. I wish we could have seen a play there; they were doing *A Midsummer Night's Dream* that evening, but all the tickets had been sold long ago. However, John is going to try to get seats for us for another night.

We were very tired when we got back, but it had been a lovely day—and I do hope John can get those tickets.

Lots of love,
LILIAN.

EXERCISES

I. *Use the following words and phrases in sentences:*

1. heavenly	8. grave	15. stage
2. typical	9. branch	16. carve
3. unlike	10. at any rate	17. long ago
4. wooden	11. jolly good	18. in the midst of
5. plant (verb)	12. leather	19. vacation
6. plant (noun)	13. pour	20. thatched
7. sculptor	14. practical	

II. *Give questions to which the following are answers.* You will find these openings helpful: "Did she?" "Is it?" "Why?" "Where?" "When?" "Has?" "What?" "Who?" "What sort of?" "Are?" "How many?"

1. Shakespeare was born in Stratford.
2. It was on April 23rd.
3. He died in 1616.
4. It is quiet, gentle scenery.
5. He bought the biggest house in Stratford.
6. It was called New Place.
7. Yes, he probably wrote *The Winter's Tale* and *The Tempest* there.
8. Because he was bad-tempered about the number of people who came to see it.
9. Andrew took a piece of the mulberry tree.
10. Because he knew Uncle Charles was very fond of Shakespeare.
11. It was carved by a Dutch sculptor.
12. No, John did not think it was good poetry.
13. No, they aren't. Each room is called by the name of a Shakespeare play.
14. No, it is quite modern.
15. Yes, it is said to be the best in England.
16. Three. Margaret, John and Andrew.
17. No, it is about as far from the sea as you can get in England.
18. She lives near Inverness in Scotland.
19. No, she went by car.
20. Yes, she said it had been a lovely day.

III. *Put in the missing words:*

1. You can't get very far from the sea — in England.
2. The scenery round Stratford is quite — the Scottish countryside — Inverness.
3. Shakespeare was — in Stratford and he — there too.
4. It seemed — that visitors should — their names on the walls.
5. In the garden grow all the flowers, trees and plants that are — in Shakespeare's — .
6. When Shakespeare became — in London, he — New Place to — to.

   7. Mr. Gastrell — the tree down.
   8. Andrew — a piece about three — — .
   9. Then we went to the church where Shakespeare is — .
  10. There are four — of poetry on Shakespeare's — .

IV. *Rearrange the following sentences, putting the words in their correct order:*

   1. you to Stratford been have ever?
   2. in yes 1955 went I
   3. winds through the slowly the river Avon town
   4. cottage about a mile Anne Hathaway's from Stratford is
   5. Hob when Stratford to went, Avon fell into the he
   6. was this funny very thought Olaf
   7. but the garden is left nothing of New Place and a few bricks
   8. well John Stratford knew Oxford because is it near quite
   9. glad in the heart was Shakespeare right I am of England born
  10. many books wrote Dickens name his and also of the house on the wall born Shakespeare where was

Composition Exercises

1. Write a letter to a friend telling him what you hope to see and do when you visit Stratford, or, if you have been there, tell him what you saw and did.

2. Describe the birthplace of a famous man in your country.

LESSON 10

Mood

MR. PRIESTLEY: Mood is the form of the verb that expresses the *manner* in which an action is done.

So far you have had two moods: (1) The **Indicative** Mood, which is used to make statements and ask questions. (2) The **Imperative** Mood, which is used to give orders or make requests.

There is a third mood, the **Subjunctive**, which is used to express a wish or a prayer that something may be or may happen, e.g.

God *save* the Queen.

This means: "I hope and pray that God will save the Queen."

Very often the Subjunctive is expressed by using one of the "special" verbs, *may* (*might*), e.g.

Long *may* she reign.

A happier time is coming. *May* I live to see it.
He wished that he *might* see happier times.

The Subjunctive has also another use; it is used in Conditional Clauses implying a negative.

OLAF: Excuse me, sir, but I don't understand what "implying a negative" means.

MR. PRIESTLEY: I am quite sure you don't, and I was just going to explain it.

Suppose, Olaf, I say to you: "If I were captain of a ship, I would take you on a voyage round the world". What do you know about me from that sentence? Do you know that I am the captain of a ship or not?

OLAF: I know that you are not a captain of a ship.

MR. PRIESTLEY: But I didn't say so.

OLAF: No; but anyone could gather that from the sentence.

MR. PRIESTLEY: I quite agree. The remark "implies" that I am not the captain. Now, Jan, here's a sentence for you:

"If John were here, he would help me with my work.

From that sentence could you say whether John is here or not?

JAN: He is not here.

MR. PRIESTLEY: But "not" is a negative word and there wasn't a "not" in my sentence.

JAN: No, there isn't a negative in it, but you gather the negative idea from the sentence.

MR. PRIESTLEY: Oh, I see. You mean that the negative is implied but not actually expressed. Let us take just one more sentence. There is a children's song that goes:

"If I were King, you should be Queen."

What is the "implied negative", Frieda?

FRIEDA: The implied negative is " . . . but he is not King" and "she is not Queen"

MR. PRIESTLEY: Now I think you all understand the point, so I will repeat what I said at first:

The Subjunctive Mood is used in Conditional Clauses implying a negative.

Here are our examples again:

Conditional Clause	Implied Negative
If I were captain of the ship If John were here If I were King	I am *not* the captain John is *not* here I am *not* King

And I want you to look again at the verbs in these conditional clauses.

If I *were* captain; if John *were* here; if I *were* King. With the pronouns *I* and *he*—both singular number—you would expect a singular verb, *am*, *is*, *was*. The form *were* is generally only used for the plural. But in the sentences I have just given you, *were* is not plural, but **Subjunctive**. That one construction *if I were*, *if you were*, *if he were*, *if they were*, etc., is practically the only example we have in modern English of the Subjunctive Mood expressed by the form of the verb.

EXERCISES

I. *Put in the correct verb (Subjunctive mood):*

1. Long — our Queen reign.
2. If I — you I would accept the offer.
3. It will be a good match. — the best man win.
4. If Hob — here, we could start the lesson.
5. Long — the Queen.
6. He wished that he — see his children again.
7. If you — the only girl in the world, and I — the only boy, there would be such wonderful things to do.
8. If they — rich they could buy a new car.
9. He is going to Italy so that he — get well again.
10. He has served his country well. — he now enjoy a happy old age.

II. *In what mood (Indicative, Imperative or Subjunctive) are the verbs in italics in the following sentences?*

1. *Are* you *coming*?
2. *Hurry* up!

3. He *is* always late.
4. *May* I *live* to see the day when he is early.
5. *Don't drop* that cup.
6. He wished that he *might get* all the sentences right.
7. To whom *must* I *give* the money?
8. The School of English *is* just past St. John's College.
9. On August 3rd I start my holiday. *May* that day *come* quickly.
10. *Put* down your pens.

III. *What are the "implied negatives" in the following sentences?*

1. If you were Henry what would you do?
2. If I were a bird I wouldn't sing in a cage.
3. If George were here he would tell us the answer.
4. "If you were the only girl in the world and I were the only boy . . ." (*Popular song.*)

What mood is were *in all those sentences? Why?*

IV. *Write five sentences containing a Conditional Clause with an implied negative.*

The Man who Didn't Like Washing Up

The following words may help you to answer the questions: *apron, blush, bowl, kitchen, mop, propose (proposal), scullery, sink* (noun), *steam, wedding*.

PICTURE 1. This is George Robinson. What is he doing? What's the difference between *washing* and *washing up*? In what room does one usually wash up? What is George holding in his right hand? What is he holding in his left hand? What is he wearing round his waist? Why? What does the water come out of? What is holding the water? What is the bowl standing in? Is the water hot or cold? How do you know? Does George look happy or unhappy? Why? What room can you see through the open door? What furniture can you see in the room?

PICTURE 2. George is looking happier; why? What thought do you think is in George's mind?

PICTURE 3. Which room is George in now? What is he doing? What do you think he is saying?

PICTURE 4. The lady is Lizzie Appleton. What is George doing now? What do you think he is saying? What colour are Lizzie's cheeks? Why? What can you say about her eyes?

PICTURE 5. What has happened? What place are they leaving? What is Lizzie carrying in her hand? What colour do you think her dress is?

PICTURE 6. Which picture is almost exactly like this one? What is the only difference?

PICTURE 1

PICTURE 2

PICTURE 3

PICTURE 4

PICTURE 5

Mervyn Wilson.

PICTURE 6

LESSON 11

Conditions

MR. PRIESTLEY: In the lesson on Adverb Clauses you were shown some Adverb Clauses of Condition like these:

Olaf will pass his examination *if he works hard.*
We will help you *if you need help.*
I cannot drink coffee *unless it is well made.*

These sentences simply mean: "If Olaf works he will pass his examination; if he doesn't, he probably won't pass." "If you ask us we will help you; if you don't ask us, then we won't help you." "If the coffee is good I can drink it; if it isn't, well, I can't." "Olaf may work hard—or he may not; you may ask for help—or you may not," and so on.

These are what we call "open conditions". Note the construction of an "open condition". In the "Condition" Clause we have the *Simple Present Tense.* In the Principal Clause we have the *Simple Future Tense.*

But there is another kind of Conditional sentence. Here are some examples set side by side with "open conditions".

A. (*Open Condition*)	B.
If Hob works hard, he will learn grammar.	If Hob worked hard, he would learn grammar.
I will help him if he asks me.	I would help him if he asked me.
He will do the work if he has time.	He would do the work if he had time.
I shall go for a walk if the rain stops.	I should go for a walk if the rain stopped.
I shall speak if I am sure of the answer.	I should speak if I were sure of the answer.

Do you notice anything about the sentences marked B, Pedro?

PEDRO: Well, the Present Tense, *work*, *help*, *will*, *shall*, has become the Past Tense, *worked*, *helped*, *would*, *should*.

MR. PRIESTLEY: Yes, quite true, but do you see anything else? Think back to our last grammar lesson. When I say: "If Hob worked hard, he would learn grammar", what do I imply?

PEDRO: Oh, I see it; you imply that he doesn't work hard. It's an "implied negative". It's like the Subjunctive!

MR. PRIESTLEY: Exactly. In fact, one of the ways of showing the Subjunctive is by using *should* and *would*. And all the other sentences are the same.

> "I would help him if he asked me" implies
> "... but he doesn't ask me".
> "... if I were sure of the answer" implies
> "... but I am not sure of the answer".

The "A" sentences are **Open Conditionals**; the "B" sentences are **Subjunctive Conditionals.**

HOB: I remember a fellow once said to me: "What would you do if you had Lord Moneybags' income?"

JAN: He implied that you hadn't an income as big as Lord Moneybags'.

HOB: I haven't!

LUCILLE: So what did you say?

HOB: I said, "What would Lord Moneybags do if he had an income like mine?"

MR. PRIESTLEY: I'll also tell you a story.

HOB: Oh yes, sir, please do.

MR. PRIESTLEY: Well, one day, when my daughter Margaret was quite a little girl, she came in to dinner with dirty hands. I said to her: "Margaret, what would you say if my hands were as dirty as yours when I came to dinner?" (implying, of course, that my hands were *not* as dirty as hers).

LUCILLE: And what did she say?

MR. PRIESTLEY: She said: "If your hands were as dirty as mine, I should be too polite to say anything about it."

FRIEDA: Margaret certainly knew what an implied negative was!

EXERCISES

I. *Put the correct verb in the blank space.*

1. I will see John if I — to Oxford.
2. If you lend me two pounds, I — pay you back tomorrow.
3. I shall go out for coffee at eleven if my essay — finished.
4. Lucille will fly to Paris if she — get a ticket.
5. If it is not too cold, I — go for a swim.
6. If he behaves badly, I — have a talk with him.
7. If you stir the sugar, the tea — be sweeter.
8. You will win much praise if you — your duty.
9. The secretary — help you if you have any difficulties.
10. I shall be very much surprised if these sandwiches — fresh.

II. *Pick out the Conditional Clauses in No. I.*

III. *Which of the following are "Open Conditionals" and which are "Subjunctive Conditionals"?*

1. If it is not foggy tomorrow, we will come.
2. If I saw him, I would speak to him.
3. I would play football if you asked me.
4. If you are right, then I am wrong.
5. If you gave that answer, you would be wrong.
6. If he spoke to me, I should speak to him.
7. If he asked for money, would you give him any?
8. Will you give him money if he asks for it?
9. If it were not so foggy, we would play football.
10. If he feels hungry, he will eat his dinner.

IV. *Rewrite the sentences of No. I as "Subjunctive Conditionals".*

LESSON 12

The Past Conditional

MR. PRIESTLEY: Do you remember, when we were studying those conditional sentences in the last grammar lesson, I asked Pedro if he noticed anything about them, and he said that the Past Tense *worked*, *helped*, *would* and *should* were used in the Subjunctive Conditionals. Well, the funny thing is that though we use a past tense, the meaning is really a present one. They mean:

. . . if Hob worked hard NOW (but he doesn't work hard NOW).

. . . if he needed help NOW (but he doesn't need help NOW).

. . . if he had time NOW.

. . . if the rain stopped NOW.

. . . if I knew the answer NOW.

In other words, all those sentences are *Present Subjunctive Conditionals*.

We can also have Subjunctive Conditionals in the Past Tense. Here is how we express the Past Conditional:

"Hob *would have learned* grammar if he *had worked* hard" (but he didn't work hard—*in the past*, and he didn't learn grammar *in the past*).

"I *would have helped* him if he *had needed* help" (but he didn't need help *in the past* and I didn't help him *in the past*).

"He *would have done* the work, if he *had had* time."

"I *should have gone* for a walk if the rain *had stopped*."

"I *should have spoken* if I *had been* sure of the answer."

86

HOB: It reminds me of an Irishman I know. A friend of his said to him: "I hear your mother-in-law has died. How long has she been dead?" The Irishman replied: "If she *had lived* till tomorrow, she *would have been dead* three months."

MR. PRIESTLEY: As you can see, we make the Past Conditional by using *would* (*should*) *have* and a past participle in the Principal Clause, and the Past Perfect Tense in the Conditional Clause.

Here are some further examples of these three constructions to help you to understand them:

Open Condition. If the master pays him properly, the workman will work well.

Present Conditional. If the master paid him properly, the workman would work well.

Past Conditional. If the master had paid him properly, the workman would have worked well.

Open Condition. If these stamps are genuine, they will be worth a lot of money.

Present Conditional. If these stamps were genuine, they would be worth a lot of money.

Past Conditional. If these stamps had been genuine, they would have been worth a lot of money.

Open Condition. If I know what you want, I will buy you a present.

Present Conditional. If I knew what you wanted, I would buy you a present.

Past Conditional. If I had known what you had wanted, I would have bought you a present.

Here it is in a "table":

		Principal Clause	*Conditional Clause*
OPEN CONDITION		he will learn	if he *works* (*Simple Present*)
S U B J U N C T I V E	PRESENT CONDITIONAL	he would learn	if he *worked* (*Simple Past*)
	PAST CONDITIONAL	he would have learned	if he had *worked* (*Past Perfect*)

EXERCISES

I. *Rewrite the following sentences* (a) *in the Present Conditional*, (b) *in the Past Conditional*. The first one is done for you.

1. I will go if you want me to.
   (*a*) I would go if you wanted me to.
   (*b*) I would have gone if you had wanted me to.
2. If you help me with the chairs, the room will soon be ready.
3. If it rains, we shan't have the picnic.
4. You will see the Eiffel Tower if you go to Paris.
5. If you have any doubts about this exercise, Mr. Priestley will help you.
6. If I receive any news, I shall let you know.

7. If you want to, we shall take a boat out on the Avon.
8. I will iron your shirt if you bring it to me.
9. If you bring that bucket, I'll fill it with water.
10. If you hit that boxer on the nose, he will hit you much harder.
11. You will become a strong man if you eat porridge.
12. If these sausages are nice, I shall go to the butcher for some more.
13. You will have rolls and coffee for breakfast if you go to the Continent.
14. If the manager is in, the secretary will tell you.
15. If the blouse matches this skirt, I will buy it.
16. If you do that, you will be all right.
17. If the cat is hungry, I will give it some food.
18. If it rains, the garden-party will be spoiled.
19. If you leave now, you will catch the train.
20. Fred will pass his examination if he works.
21. I will give him the money if I see him.
22. If you drink that, it will kill you.
23. The boy will post your letter if you give it to him.
24. It will be safer if you don't give him the money.
25. If you don't wear a thick coat, you will be very cold.

TEST PAPER No. 1

I. *Put the verbs in the following sentences in their corresponding past tense and name the tense.*

1. I think I can have lunch on the train.
2. The building is very ugly and I can never live in it.
3. I have 2½ pence to spend.
4. You are doing this exercise well.
5. He gives me so much that I feel I can't repay him.
6. Do you wish to marry my daughter?
7. I am hoping that the weather will be fine.
8. Hob gets the sentence wrong, but he's still cheerful.

D

9. You will finish your work by nine o'clock. (*Use Future Perfect tense.*)

10. I don't expect that my painting will win a prize.

II. *Turn the following into Indirect Speech:*

1. Mr. Priestley asked, "Are all my students here?"
2. Joe said, "That car will cost a lot of money."
3. Lucille said, "I know where I can get a cheaper one."
4. The porter said, "I have put your luggage on the train."
5. Pedro asked, "How much is that blue suit?"
6. THE TEACHER TO THE BOYS: "Open your books."
7. ANDREW: "When will tea be ready?"
8. MRS. PRIESTLEY TO THE BAKER: "Don't leave any bread to-morrow."
9. Grandma said, "I am having trouble with my false teeth."
10. PEDRO TO THE WAITER: "Why isn't this tablecloth clean?"

III. *Join these two sentences, by using a relative pronoun instead of the word in italics (e.g.* I have bought a new car. I paid £540 for *it.* I have bought a new car for *which* I paid £540).

1. This is Olaf. *He* arrived at Newcastle this morning.
2. Here's the book. I told you about *it.*
3. That hen has escaped again. You ate *its* egg for breakfast.
4. Look at the blackbird. We heard *him* singing this morning.
5. What is the name of that lady? *She* always dresses charmingly.
6. Where is my money? I left *it* here last night.
7. You can collect the tickets from the booking office. I paid for *them* yesterday.
8. Andrew goes to a boarding-school. *The school* has a good reputation.
9. I went to the college in Oxford last week-end. I used to live in *it.*
10. Put it in the book-case. *The book-case* stands by the fireplace.

IV. (a) *Pick out the subordinate clause from these sentences.*
   (b) *Say whether it is a noun or adverb clause.*
   (c) *Rewrite the sentence in the past tense.*

   1. He says these sentences will be easy.
   2. What you are writing is all wrong.
   3. Because my passport hasn't come, I have to spend the night at Harwich.
   4. I lock the door so that a burglar can't get in.
   5. He promises that it won't happen again.

V. *Complete the following sentences in your own words:*

   1. Unless . . . I shan't come to this hotel again.
   2. As soon as the meal was finished, Hob . . .
   3. I don't think that . . .
   4. After . . . the aerodrome was silent.
   5. The actress is so bad-tempered that . . .
   6. If I were Prime Minister . . .
   7. You should have known that . . .
   8. . . . so that I should not miss the plane for Berne.
   9. May you live to see the day . . .
   10. We shall go for a bathe, if . . .

VI. (a) *What is an "implied negative"? Give an example.*
   (b) *What are the names of three moods? Give an example of each.*
   (c) *Put the correct form of the verb in these sentences, and say what mood the verb is in:*

   1. Don't (leave) me to do all the work.
   2. If you (eat) so much, you will be ill.
   3. If I (be) you, I should be very careful.
   4. God (save) the Queen.
   5. (Go) home at once!

6. Where (be) the money you promised me?
7. You would never have known if I (not tell) you.
8. I (study) English for three years now.

VII. *Contradict these remarks* (*e.g.* " It rained yesterday." " No, it didn't "). *Use shortened forms.*

1. John is at Cambridge.
2. Hob can't eat the breakfast.
3. The painter paid three pounds.
4. Jan doesn't like Frieda.
5. I'm not going to get up yet.
6. You didn't do that exercise very well.
7. The last train has gone.
8. Mrs. Priestley takes sugar in her tea.
9. I shall leave here at six o'clock.
10. They hadn't washed the dishes.

VIII. *Write questions to which the following replies
may be given:*

1. No, I don't.
2. It has stopped raining.
3. 22½ pence, sir.
4. Yes, if you hurry.
5. It's a quarter to four.
6. You can get a good cup at Susan's Café.
7. The 14 bus will take you there.
8. He's called Jock.
9. Yes, if you want to.
10. That's Big Ben.

IX.   *Composition Exercise*

Write about 200 words on one of the following:

(*a*) A Visit to a Big City.
(*b*) A Sea Voyage.
(*c*) The Wiggins Family.

X. *Read the following passage carefully and then answer the questions below:*

Since his retirement Uncle George had become a frequent visitor at art exhibitions, and Aunt Judith was pleased not only because it did not cost much but also because it made a good impression on the neighbours. However, after a time, Uncle, not content with just looking at the pictures, began to buy them and his wife's pleasure grew less.

What happened when Uncle returned home with his latest picture was always the same. Aunt Judith's welcome used to die on her lips as she saw the large parcel under his arm, but Uncle never seemed to notice. He would rush past his wife, place the parcel on the hall table and with excited fingers begin to untie the knots.

(1) *Give another word or phrase of similar meaning to the following as they are used in the passage:*

(a) Since his retirement
(b) had become a frequent visitor
(c) neighbours
(d) place
(e) parcel

(2) *Why was Aunt Judith pleased when her husband began to go to art exhibitions?*

(3) *Why did she become less pleased later?*

(4) *What did the "large parcel" contain?*

(5) *Mention two things in the second paragraph that show the very great interest that Uncle George had in art.*

LESSON 13

"Should" and "Would"

MR. PRIESTLEY: Let us now gather together all the uses of *should* and *would*.

(1) They are used as the Past Tense of *shall* and *will* to show "future in the past" (page 19).

(2) They are used to show "Subjunctive Conditional" implying a negative.

Those are the two uses that we have studied. But there are others:

(3) *Should* is used to show a **duty** or an **obligation.** Here it has the meaning of *ought*, e.g.

You *should* do better work than this (= you ought to do better work than this).

If he left here at four o'clock he *should* (= ought to) be home by now.

The students *should* (= ought to) know by now that the teacher won't accept bad work.

You shouldn't (= oughtn't to) eat peas with a knife.

HOB: One day I heard Aunt Aggie talking to a workman. She said: "When I use a hammer I always hit my thumb with it. What *should* I do to prevent that?" He said: "The only thing that I can think of, madam, is that you *should* hold the hammer with both hands."

PEDRO: I knew a poet (not a very good poet) who said to a friend: "Do you think I *should* put more fire into my poems?" His friend said: "No, I really think you *should* put more of your poems in the fire."

HOB: Oh, I must tell you about my young cousin, Ted. One day he came downstairs crying loudly. "What's the matter now?" I said. "Father was hanging a picture and hit his thumb with the hammer," said Ted. "Well," I said, "that's not serious. A big boy like you *shouldn't* cry about a little thing like that. Why don't you laugh?"

"I did," said Ted.

MR. PRIESTLEY: We also express the idea of past obligation or duty by means of *should* and the Perfect Infinitive, like this:

"You *should have done* better work than this."
(= You ought to have done better work than this.)
"You *should have known* by now that the teacher won't accept bad work."
"You *shouldn't have eaten* your peas with a knife."

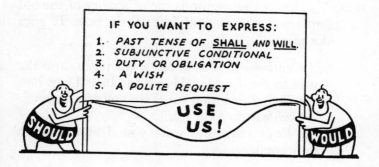

IF YOU WANT TO EXPRESS:
1. PAST TENSE OF <u>SHALL</u> *AND* <u>WILL</u>.
2. SUBJUNCTIVE CONDITIONAL
3. DUTY OR OBLIGATION
4. A WISH
5. A POLITE REQUEST

SHOULD

USE US!

WOULD

Or, to take Hob's story:

"What *should I have done* to prevent that?"
"You *should have held* the hammer with both hands."

(4) *Should* and *would* are used to express a wish, e.g.

We *should like* to know what he is going to do next (= we wish we knew what . . .).

I *should like* you to play some Chopin for me (= I wish you would . . .).

Hob *would like* to know when this lesson is going to end. (he wishes he knew when . . .).

(5) *Would* is sometimes used in making requests (especially in the phrase "Would you mind . . .?") because we feel it is rather more polite than a direct Imperative or *will*, e.g.

"*Would* you shut the door, please?"
(*Imperative*—Shut the door, please. With "*will*". Will you shut the door, please?)
Would you mind opening the window, please?
Would you mind passing me the salt?

HOB: You know that reminds me of a story of the old gentleman and the impolite little boy. It goes like this:

Old Gentleman: Would you mind telling me the way to the London Home for Lost Dogs?
Little Boy: It's a long way; are you in a hurry?
Old Gentleman: Yes, I am.
Little Boy: Then, if I were you, I *should* bite a policeman.

MR. PRIESTLEY : There is just one other use of *should* and *would* that I want to mention.

(6) They are sometimes used in an Adverbial Clause of Purpose, e.g.

"I got up early, so that I *should not* be late for the train."
"Hob had a good breakfast, so that *he wouldn't* feel hungry before 11 o'clock."

And that's enough of *should* and *would*.

EXERCISES

I. *Rewrite the following sentences using "should" instead of "ought to":*

1. He ought to work much harder.
2. Aunt Aggie ought to hold the hammer with both hands.
3. You oughtn't to cry about a little thing like that.
4. The children ought to be asleep by now.
5. That bicycle ought to be big enough for you.
6. Hob ought to have passed that exam.
7. My doctor says that I oughtn't to lift heavy things.
8. You oughtn't to have smoked a cigarette in class.
9. What ought Ted to have done, when his father hit his thumb?
10. He ought to have kept quiet.
11. You ought to see a Shakespeare play if you go to Stratford.
12. Mr. Wiggins really ought to buy a new car.
13. The boy ought to be punished.
14. All these papers ought not to be left on the ground.
15. I really ought to get on with my work.

II. *Put "would" or "should" in the blank spaces:*

1. I — like to hear that song again.
2. Do you think I — take a holiday.
3. No, it — be better if you got on with your work.

   4. — you mind carving the meat?

   5. The boys — play more quietly.

   6. The fire — have burned better, if I had had more wood.

   7. If I were you, I — go for a bathe now.

   8. I — like to know when we will have breakfast.

   9. My landlady — not try to make coffee.

  10. He worked hard so that he — pass the exam.

III. *Rewrite these sentences in a polite way, beginning with "Would you mind . . .?" and ending with "please" (e.g. Come here. — Would you mind coming here, please?)*

   1. Open the window.

   2. Stop the car.

   3. Get on with your work.

   4. Tell Timothy to come here at once.

   5. Talk less loudly.

   6. Go away.

   7. Hold this hammer.

   8. Help me with the chairs.

   9. Repeat that sentence.

  10. Pay at the booking-office.

Composition Exercises

Write or tell the story of:

  (*a*) Auntie Aggie and the Workman.

  (*b*) Ted and the Hammer.

  (*c*) The Old Gentleman and the Impolite Little Boy.

LESSON 14

Olaf Gives us Another "Wiggins" Play

OLAF: I've written another little play about the Wiggins family and I've tried to use a lot of examples of *should* and *would*. May I read it to you?

MR. PRIESTLEY: We should enjoy that very much.

OLAF: Thank you. Here's the play.

A Visit to the Cinema

Scene: THE DRAWING-ROOM AT THE WIGGINS' HOUSE

MR. WIGGINS: Ah, a chair by the fire at last. It's nice to sit down and take it easy after a hard day's work.

GRANDMA: You wouldn't be so pleased if you had to sit here all day long like Grandpa and me.

MRS. WIGGINS: Well, Grandma, what would you like to do?

GRANDMA: I'd like to go to the pictures.

MR. WIGGINS: You wouldn't if you looked out of the window. It's pouring with rain.

MRS. WIGGINS: Then you should offer to take them in the car, James.

MR. WIGGINS: I've just put the car away. Grandma should make up her mind earlier if she wants to go to the pictures.

99

GRANDPA: Did I hear James say that he would take us to the pictures?

MRS. WIGGINS: Yes, Grandpa. As it's raining he'll take you in the car. He thought it would be a change for you.

TIMOTHY: I want to go to the pictures too.

MRS. WIGGINS: You can't go tonight, dear. The pictures won't finish till long past your bedtime.

MR. WIGGINS: It will finish past mine too. I was looking forward to an early night.

MRS. WIGGINS: Now don't be selfish, James. Grandma and Grandpa get little enough pleasure from life, as it is.

GRANDPA: And sitting in this room with the walls painted green isn't one of them. I would have painted them red.

GRANDMA: Yes, red would have been much better. Are you going to take us, James, or not?

MR. WIGGINS: Well, what's on at the pictures?

MRS. WIGGINS: It should be in the local paper. Ah yes, here we are. "The Secret Life of Walter Mitty", starring Danny Kaye.

MR. WIGGINS: I've seen that once already.

GRANDMA: Ah, Grandpa always says that the only way to appreciate a picture properly is to see it twice, don't you, Grandpa?

GRANDPA: Yes, always.

MRS. WIGGINS: Well, I'm sure you will all enjoy it. Timothy, go and get Grandma's coat, and you must go and get the car started, James. We don't want to keep Grandma waiting.

*　　　*　　　*　　　*

(Half an hour later. In the Cinema)

MR. WIGGINS: Well, here we are.

GRANDMA: And we're lucky to be here in one piece. The way you came round that corner was most dangerous.

MR. WIGGINS: Well, I knew you wouldn't want to be late.

GRANDMA: Ah, Grandpa always made a joke about that. He always said, "It's better to be 'late' than 'the late'."

MR. WIGGINS: I know. You've told me before.

GRANDMA: Well, one wouldn't think so from the way you drove us here.

GRANDPA: How long must we go on waiting, listening to that dreadful music.

MR. WIGGINS: The main picture starts in two minutes.

GRANDMA: This isn't a very good seat. It would be better if Grandpa moved up to the next one. Tell him to move up, James.

MR. WIGGINS: He wouldn't be very comfortable if he did.

GRANDMA: Why not?

MR. WIGGINS: Someone's sitting there.

GRANDMA: Have you any chocolates?

MR. WIGGINS: No.

GRANDMA: Oh, what a pity. Grandpa would never take someone to the pictures without buying a box of chocolates, would you, Grandpa?

GRANDPA: What's that?

GRANDMA: I was saying you always bought a box of chocolates.

GRANDPA: Chocolates? Yes, I would like a chocolate.

GRANDMA: We haven't any. James has forgotten.

MR. WIGGINS: Be quiet. The picture's starting.

GRANDMA: I shan't see much of it from this seat. You should have bought us better seats, James.

MR. WIGGINS: Oh, look at the picture.

GRANDMA: Who's that young man with red hair. I've seen him somewhere before.

MR. WIGGINS: I expect so. He's a well-known star.

GRANDPA: Have you noticed he drives a car just like James, Grandma?

GRANDMA: Yes, you're right, Grandpa. Very dangerous. He's behaving very queerly altogether. He's nothing like the fine handsome film stars of my day; you should have seen . . .

MR. WIGGINS: I wish you wouldn't talk so much. The people in front are looking round.

GRANDMA: Well, ask that lady in front of me if she would mind taking her hat off. She seems to have a bowl of fruit on her head.

MR. WIGGINS: Change seats with me. I can see perfectly.

(*They change seats. Two minutes later*)

GRANDMA: James, I've seen this picture before.

MR. WIGGINS: Well, so have I. I thought you enjoyed seeing a picture twice.

GRANDMA: Don't be silly. Who would want to see the same picture twice? We're going home. I can't think why you dragged us away from a warm fire to see a film that we've already seen. We should have been far better at home. Come along, Grandpa, come along, James!

EXERCISES

I. *Use the following words and phrases in sentences:*

1. offer
2. pour
3. selfish
4. local
5. appreciate
6. lucky
7. dreadful
8. dangerous
9. pity
10. queerly
11. drag
12. silly
13. seat
14. take it easy
15. in front

II. *Put the following sentences into indirect speech:*

1. Mr. Wiggins said, "It's nice to sit down after a hard day's work."
2. TIMOTHY: "Take us to the pictures, Father."
3. MR. WIGGINS: "It's pouring with rain."
4. MRS. WIGGINS: "Can't you take them in the car?"
5. MR. WIGGINS: "I've just put the car away."
6. GRANDMA: "Get the car out again."
7. HOB: "I'm glad I don't live with Grandma Wiggins."
8. OLAF TO HOB: "I expect Grandma is glad she doesn't live with you."
9. JOHN PRIESTLEY: "Come to see me in Oxford."
10. MRS. PRIESTLEY TO FRIEDA: "May I give you a cup of tea before you go?"
11. PEDRO: "It always pays to go to a good tailor."
12. HOB: "I always pay when I go to any sort of tailor."

13. GRANDMA: "I've seen this picture before."
14. LUCILLE: "How much is that coat?"
15. FRIEDA: "I hope Jan will come with me."

III. *Begin the following sentences with "it", and keep the meaning the same by using the infinitive (e.g. "Sitting in this room is no pleasure to me."—"It is no pleasure to me to sit in this room").*

1. Seeing a picture twice is not my idea of fun.
2. Doing these exercises is excellent practice.
3. Driving a car at night is not always easy.
4. Reading a book by the fire is pleasant after a hard day's work.
5. Climbing mountains is sometimes dangerous.
6. Telling jokes is one of Hob's great joys.
7. Doing these exercises is not always as easy as it looks.

IV. *Answer the following:*

1. Why did Mr. Wiggins say it was nice to sit down?
2. Why did Grandma disagree?
3. What was the weather like?
4. Grandpa was rather deaf. Find two instances of it in this play.
5. What did Mr. Wiggins mean by an "early night"?
6. Why couldn't Timothy go to the pictures?
7. What is a "local paper"?
8. What is "a film star"? Mention three by name.
9. What colour would Grandpa have painted the walls?
10. What entertainment was there in the cinema before the picture started? How do you know?
11. Why couldn't Grandpa move up to the next seat?
12. What did Grandma think of Mr. Wiggins' driving?
13. What did the hat of the lady in front remind Grandma of?
14. What was the name of "that young man with red hair"?
15. Why did Grandma decide to go home?

V. *What is the difference between:*

1. a car and a van.
2. a chair and a seat.
3. a picture and a cinema.
4. handsome and pretty.
5. late and "the late".
6. a minute and an hour.
7. warm and hot?

Composition Exercises

1. Tell or write:

   (*a*) The story of Mr. Wiggins' visit to the cinema.

   (*b*) The story of any film you have seen.

2. Who is your favourite film star ? Why ? What parts does he or she play well ?

LESSON 15

Rules of Grammar and "Standard English"

JAN: There is one thing that rather puzzles me. You have given us from time to time a "rule" of grammar, or sometimes we are told, "That is not good grammar." Who makes the "rules" of grammar? Who decides whether a sentence is right or wrong?

MR. PRIESTLEY: No one.

JAN: But isn't there an Academy that does it?

MR. PRIESTLEY: Not in England.

LUCILLE: Hasn't Oxford University or Cambridge anything to do with it?

MR. PRIESTLEY: No. You see, the grammar of a language is not a list of rules forced on the people who speak it; it is just a record made by careful observation of how the people speak the language.

PEDRO: But you have "rules" and laws of grammar to say "this is right and this is wrong". Surely the language must obey these rules?

MR. PRIESTLEY: You have "rules and laws of Nature", but these are not rules for Nature that Nature has to obey, they are just a few things that wise men have observed as to the way Nature acts. If we find that Nature is not acting according to these rules we don't try to force Nature to obey them; we change the rules and make new ones.

LUCILLE: And is it the same with grammar?

MR. PRIESTLEY: Exactly. Language is a living thing, always changing; old words die, new words come in; some constructions gradually fall out of use, others push their way in. The English of today is not quite the same as the English of the eighteenth century; the English of King Alfred[1] could not be understood at all by Englishmen of today. What was good grammar for Shakespeare could be bad grammar for Shaw.

PEDRO: To come back to this question of what is grammatically "right" and what is grammatically "wrong": how do you decide?

MR. PRIESTLEY: Whatever form is used by the majority of educated speakers or writers is correct; or, as Sweet[2] puts it, "Whatever is in general use in a language is, for that reason, grammatically correct." That is all.

FRIEDA: Is what you have said about grammar true also about pronunciation?

MR. PRIESTLEY: Yes. Pronunciation has changed, and is changing constantly.

JAN: It must be more difficult to decide what is right and what is wrong in pronunciation than it is in grammar, for in different parts of England there are different pronunciations.

OLAF: Yes, I noticed that. In Scotland the pronunciation is quite different from the London one.

[1] A.D. 849–901.
[2] Henry Sweet 1845–1912), a famous writer on the English language.

FRIEDA: I noticed that, too, in Devon.

HOB: My uncle Albert speaks with a Lancashire accent. It seems to me that almost every part of England has a different pronunciation.

MR. PRIESTLEY: Yes, you are not far wrong. And if you are considering different kinds of English, you might have included the English spoken in Wales, Scotland, Ireland, Australia, South Africa, New Zealand, Canada and the United States.

LUCILLE: Well, where is the best English spoken? That is, naturally, the one we want to learn to speak and write.

MR. PRIESTLEY: I think I am asked that question by every class that I teach. From the point of view of the student of language there is no form that is better than any other. The best Devonshire English is spoken in Devon, the purest Scottish English in Scotland, the most correct London English in London and the best American English in the United States.

PEDRO: I see. But which type of English must we learn?

MR. PRIESTLEY: Ah, that's rather another matter. The most convenient form, and the one I am teaching you, is that used by the great majority of educated speakers in South and South-east England, especially in London and its neighbourhood. It is used, too, in most of the universities and public schools in England. It is easily understood in all parts of the English-speaking world. It is, at the present time, more widely spoken than any other form and, owing to the spread of education and the influence of the B.B.C., whose announcers use this form, it is getting more widespread every day. For that reason and from that point of view you can, if you like, call it "Standard" English.

HOB: Well, if it's good enough for the B.B.C. it's good enough for me.

JAN: Could you tell us more, some time, about Standard English? There's a lot more I want to know.

FRIEDA: So do I. Not only about Standard English but about the English language generally.

LUCILLE: Such as — ?

JAN: Well, such things as: "Why doesn't everyone in England speak Standard English?"

OLAF: And, "Is Standard English the same as the 'King's (or Queen's) English'?"

JAN: Yes, and "Why does Standard English seem to belong to the South of England rather than the North?"

PEDRO: And, "Do all speakers of Standard English speak the same?" I mention this because I think I have heard differences between your pronunciation, Mr. Priestley, and your son John's.

MR. PRIESTLEY: You have certainly given me some questions to answer, and I shall be very pleased to deal with them all at some later date.

EXERCISES

I. *Use the following words and phrases in sentences:*

1. puzzle	6. educated	11. influence
2. whether	7. constantly	12. B.B.C.
3. obey	8. naturally	13. at the present time
4. according to	9. majority	14. widespread
5. gradually	10. Public Schools	15. convenient

II. *Make verbs from the following nouns: the words needed are all in this lesson. Use each of these nouns and each of the verbs that you make from them in a sentence:*

1. obedience. 2. pronunciation. 3. influence. 4. decision. 5. speech. 6. student. 7. trial. 8. explanation. 9. thought. 10. death. 11. record. 12. difference.

Make adjectives from numbers 1, 3, 4, 6, 8, 9, 10 *and* 12, *and adverbs from numbers* 1, 3, 4, 6, 9 *and* 12. *Use each adjective and adverb in a sentence.*

III. *Express the following words and phrases in one word. You are given the first letter and number of letters in the word. All the words come from this lesson.*

1. to become different, not to stay the same. (c – – – – –)
2. the opposite of *live*. (d – –)
3. the opposite of *easy*. (d – – – – – – – –)
4. one hundred years. (c – – – – – –)
5. a law. (r – – –)
6. right, not wrong. (c – – – – – –)
7. to be ruled by, to do as you are told. (o – – –)
8. unlike, not the same. (d – – – – – – – –)
9. sort (*noun*). (t – – –)

10. instruction. (e – – – – – – – –)
11. found in a great many places. (w – – – – – – – – –)
12. nearly. (a – – – – –)

IV. *Answer these questions:*

1. Who made the rules of grammar?
2. What is Standard English?
3. Why does Mr. Priestley teach it?
4. What does he mean when he says "Language is a living thing"?
5. What is an accent?
6. Why is Standard English becoming more widely spoken?
7. What did Mr. Priestley reply when asked where the best English was spoken?
8. Mention five countries not in the British Isles where English is spoken.
9. When was King Alfred born?
10. What two writers of plays are mentioned in this lesson?

Composition Exercise

What do you think of the B.B.C.? Write about some of the programmes you have heard and compare them with the radio programmes of your own country.

LESSON 16

Lucille's Story: "The Sand-glass"

LUCILLE: It's usually Hob who has the interesting relatives, Aunt Aggie, Uncle Tom, Albert, Theophilus—to mention just a few of them, but, though it is not about an actual relative, I could tell you a story about my old nurse Anna. May I do so?

MR. PRIESTLEY: We should be delighted to listen to you, Lucille. Please tell us the story.

LUCILLE: Well, Anna was a dear old servant in our house in Paris. She had been a servant in our family before I was born and had been nurse to my sisters Marie and Yvonne and to me. She helped with the work in the house, she did the sewing, she could cook an omelette, or any other dish, better than anyone else I know. We all loved her, she was so kind, so helpful and so constantly busy. From early morning till late at night she never rested and nothing was too much trouble for her. If ever we were in difficulties, from a torn frock to a broken heart, it was to Anna that we went for help and comfort.

Then, one day, she came to say that she was leaving us. "Leaving us, Anna!" I said, hardly able to believe my ears.

"Yes, Miss Lucille," she said, and then, blushing and looking rather confused, she said, "I'm going to be married." You could, as Hob said, have knocked me down with a feather. Because we had known her all our lives, we girls naturally thought of Anna as old, but I don't suppose she was more than forty when she left us; for she did leave us, and married Henri Behr.

It was the greatest mistake she ever made in her life, and, though Anna never said a word about it, I am sure she regretted it almost from the day she was married. Anna had saved quite a bit of money during the years she had been with us, and with it she bought a house in Tours. It was quite a big old house, and she made her living by letting rooms in it. And when I say *she* made the living, I mean that, for Henri did absolutely nothing at all. My father and mother and my sisters and I at some time or other all visited Anna, but none of us liked Henri. He was ten or twelve years older than Anna, a big, unpleasant, selfish, bad-tempered man. I never once saw him smile or say a kind word to anyone. But all this was nothing compared with his laziness. That was almost beyond belief. I don't think he had ever done a stroke of work in his life. He certainly never did after he married Anna. He got up about ten o'clock in the morning (by which time Anna had been up for four or five hours) and sat in his armchair by the big stove, and there he would sit until it was time to go to bed. Anna had to leave her work and

hurry to bring him his breakfast of rolls and
butter and coffee. Then he sat and read his
paper and smoked his pipe or slept while Anna
ran about upstairs cleaning all the rooms (and
with Anna everything was always as clean and
bright as a new pin), making the beds, doing the
washing, or running downstairs half a dozen
times to answer the door-bell. And in the midst
of it all she had to prepare the vegetables and
cook the huge meal that he always expected
promptly at one o'clock. A dozen times a day
you would hear him shout, "Anna", and she
had to leave her work and hurry to see what he
wanted. It would usually be to pick up the
pipe that he had dropped, or find another
cushion for his head, get him a glass of wine or
put some more wood on the fire. If she didn't
come running the moment he called, he would
burst into a fit of rage, his face would go red with
anger and you could hear his shouting all over
the house.

Well, for the next year or two we lost touch
with Anna. Tours is a hundred and fifty miles
or so from Paris, and in any case we hated to see
her so unhappy, so we never went to see her.
Then, one day, I went to Tours to visit some
friends and I thought I would call and see Anna.
I went to the house where she lived near the
Church of Notre-Dame-la-Riche. I rang the
bell—it was one of those old-fashioned ones that
you pulled—and I could hear it ringing through
the house. I waited, but there was no sound of

footsteps in the house. I waited, perhaps for two minutes, but still all was silent. But the house was occupied; there was smoke coming from the chimney (it was in December), and I recognised Anna's clean, bright curtains in the windows. I rang again, louder than before, and then, after another minute or so, I heard footsteps slowly coming down the stairs. The door opened and I saw Anna. The moment she saw me her face lighted up with a smile. I threw my arms round her and said, "Oh, Anna, how nice to see you again!" There was no doubt about her joy at seeing me. She took me upstairs to her cosy room, neat and clean and tidy as Anna's rooms always were. The room was exactly as I had always known it—except that Henri wasn't there. Oh, yes, and except for one other thing. On the table near Anna's chair (the chair where Henri always used to sit) was a big sand-glass, I think you call it an egg-timer.

FRIEDA: I know what you mean. The sand takes four minutes to run through from the top to the bottom of the glass; and that's the time you need to boil an egg.

OLAF: I saw a big one like that in an old church in Scotland. But they called them "hour-glasses". The sand took an hour to run through, and when the preacher began his sermon he used to turn the glass upside down and then he preached until all the sand had run through. Those old Scots liked good value for their money!

HOB: Never mind the Scots. Let Lucille get on with her story. I want to hear what happened to Henri. I think Anna had murdered him; I hope she had.

LUCILLE: Well, I noticed that Anna looked every now and then at the sand-glass and whenever she saw that the sand (a peculiar, dark-coloured sand) had run through, she turned the glass and let the sand run through again. Just then the front door-bell rang again, but instead of jumping up at once to answer it as Anna always used to do, she just turned the sand-glass over and sat still. When the sand had all run through, she got up quietly and went downstairs to answer the door. So that was why I had had to wait so long! It all seemed very funny, but I didn't say anything. She came back and we continued our chat, and then she said, "But you must be hungry, Miss Lucille; I'll make lunch. Would you like an omelette?" I certainly was hungry and, knowing Anna's omelette of old, I said there was nothing I should like better. But again she didn't get up. She just turned over the sand-glass and when she saw the sand had run through, she got up and cooked the lunch. It was not until we had finished lunch that I said, "Where's Henri?" Anna said, "He's dead; he died about a year ago." I couldn't say, "I'm sorry to hear it," I just sat silent. Anna continued, "He got into one of his rages and suddenly dropped down dead." There was a pause. She picked up the sand-glass. "I had him cremated," she said. "These," and she pointed to the sand, "are his ashes. He never worked while he was alive, but I see to it that he does now he's dead."

And she turned the sand-glass over again.

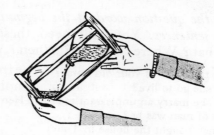

EXERCISES

I. *Use the following words and phrases in sentences:*

1. actual
2. delight
3. nurse
4. torn
5. comfort
6. in difficulties
7. beyond belief
8. laziness
9. a stroke of work
10. prompt
11. cushion
12. a fit of rage
13. we lost touch with
14. old-fashioned
15. occupied
16. neat
17. tidy
18. cosy
19. preach
20. sermon
21. value
22. murder
23. peculiar
34. omelette
25. cremate

II. *Put the verbs into the correct tense:*

1. How long (you know) Anna?
2. She (stay) with our family for twenty years.
3. After her marriage we (not see) her for a long time.
4. I (visit) Tours a few months ago.
5. We (be) at Victoria in ten minutes.
6. It (be) ten years since I (leave) school.

7. We (not see) John for two months.
8. How long (you stay) in England?
9. Olaf (finish) that exercise five minutes ago.
10. I (not be) to Lisbon since the war.

III. *Put in the question word at the beginning of the following sentences.* You will need these words: Why? What? Where? Whose? When? Which?

1. — was the name of your old nurse?
2. — did she go to live?
3. — did she marry an unpleasant man like Henri?
4. — sort of man was he?
5. — money bought the house in Tours?
6. — will you be ready?
7. — are you doing?
8. — have you changed your clothes?
9. — is my tie? I can't find it.
10. — train shall we catch? The four o'clock or the five-thirty?

IV. *Write the following sentences using* else *instead of* other. These are the phrases you will need: nothing else, everyone else, no one else, someone else, anything else, somewhere else. No. 1 is done for you.

1. She is a better cook than any other person I know. (She is a better cook than anyone else I know.)
2. Hob asked if there was any other thing for lunch.
3. Do you want to see Olaf or some other person?
4. Every other person thought Henri was lazy and unpleasant.
5. He sat and read his paper, but never did any other thing.
6. Hob got it wrong, but every other person got it right.
7. Shakespeare was a great writer, and there is no other person like him.

8. My pen is not on my desk. I must have left it in some other place.

9. I wanted to use the phone but some other person was using it.

10. I want some two-inch nails, and no other things will do.

V. *Answer these questions:*

1. How long had Lucille known Anna?
2. What was the greatest mistake Anna ever made?
3. What sort of a man was Henri Behr?
4. What time did Anna usually get up after she was married?
5. Why did Lucille's family stop visiting Anna?
6. What two things were different when Lucille visited Anna's home again?
7. Why were sand-glasses used in some Scottish churches?
8. How did Anna make Henri work after he was dead?

VI. *Give another word or phrase of similar meaning to the following:*

1. delighted	6. rage	11. I'll see to it
2. blushing	7. occupied	12. suddenly
3. regretted	8. joy	13. a pause
4. a dozen	9. murder (verb)	14. a chat
5. a sermon	10. continue	15. peculiar

Composition Exercises

1. Tell or write the story of Anna's marriage to Henri.

2. Write a letter to a friend who wants a cook, telling him about Anna, and suggesting she would suit him.

LESSON 17

"Rules of Grammar" Again

JAN: You spoke to us in one lesson about "rules of grammar". Well, I was looking at a grammar book (not one of yours) and on one page it gave some teaching about the use of *whom*. I don't think you have said anything to us about this, but some of the sentences it gave, and especially a rule that it added, seemed rather strange to me. It said, for example:

"A common mistake that students make is to say:

Who do you want to see?
Who is he speaking to?
Who did you play with?

These should be:

Whom do you want to see?
Whom is he speaking to?
Whom did you play with?

or, better still for the second and third ones:

To whom is he speaking?
With whom did you play?

These forms are better because a preposition is generally placed immediately before the noun or pronoun that it governs, and you ought not to end a sentence with a preposition."

What is your opinion, sir?

MR. PRIESTLEY: Let us take the point about *whom* first. The relative pronoun and the interrogative pronoun *who* has three forms: *who* (nominative), *whom* (objective), *whose* (possessive). Here are examples of each:

RELATIVE PRONOUN

That is the man *who* spoke to me.
That is the man *whom* I spoke to.
or   That is the man to *whom* I spoke.
That is the man *whom* I saw.
That is the man *whose* house was burnt down.

INTERROGATIVE PRONOUN

Who is speaking now?
Whom do you want to see?
Whom are you looking at?
Whose is this book, yours or mine?

Now in writing, and perhaps in formal speaking, we use *whom* when the relative pronoun or the interrogative pronoun is in the objective case. But in conversation, especially in informal colloquial[1] speech, most people would use the interrogative pronoun *who* instead of *whom*. They would say, for example:

Who do you want to see?
Who did you speak to?
Who are you looking at?

---

[1] Don't mistake *colloquial speech* for *slang*. Colloquial speech is the kind of speech that educated English people would use in natural, informal talk.

E

If the relative pronoun is in the objective case
and if it is a defining relative, it is usually omitted
in colloquial speech, e.g.

That's the man I spoke to.
That's the man I saw.

＊   ＊   ＊   ＊

Now let us come to the second point, the
"rule":

"Never end a sentence with a preposition."

That is just nonsense. Practically every great
writer and every speaker of English has broken
that rule; in fact there are some prepositions[1]
which are used in phrases that can only be put
at the end of the sentence. They are usually
prepositions that are closely associated with
verbs. For example:

It was worth *waiting for*. It's not a thing to
laugh about. When I went swimming, I handed
him my watch *to take care of*. Bread is a thing we
can't *do without*.

HOB : Sir, I know a story about ending sentences with
prepositions.

MR. PRIESTLEY : Hob, there seems to be nothing you
don't know stories about. (And there's another
end preposition!) But let us have it by all means.

HOB : It's about Sir Winston Churchill when he was
Prime Minister of England. He had written out
an important speech that he was going to give,
and he handed it to one of his secretaries to type.
When he got it back he found that the secretary

---

[1] Many of these prepositions have an adverbial force.

had gone through the speech and changed all the sentences that ended with a preposition. Sir Winston marked all these alterations in red ink and wrote underneath:

"This is the sort of English up with which I will not put."

MR. PRIESTLEY: Very good, Hob. But there is a story about the funny effect you get if you get too many end prepositions.

HOB: Oh, sir, tell us the story.

MR. PRIESTLEY: Well, it's about a very small boy who couldn't read. He asked his mother to read to him, so she went to get a book; but it was not the one he wanted, and as soon as he saw it he said:

"Oh, Mummy, what did you bring me that book to be read *to out of for*?"

PEDRO: Are there any occasions when you mustn't have the "end preposition"?

MR. PRIESTLEY: Yes, there are. Here is one:

"The unwillingness *with which Hob comes* to a grammar lesson, and the speed *with which he goes away from it*, have always amused me." You couldn't say "The unwillingness he comes to a grammar lesson *with*" and "the speed he goes away from it *with*."[1]

And now to end this lesson I want to tell you about a conversation that I took part in (or "in which I took part"). It was with Professor Grey. He's a Professor of Ancient Languages. He knows so much about ancient languages that I

---

[1] But this could be expressed more neatly by saying "Hob's unwillingness in coming . . . and his speed in going away . . ."

think he always lives in the past. He also has some very fixed ideas about English. My new book on "Colloquial English" had just been published, and I happened to meet him on the station when we were both going in to London.

"Oh, Priestley," he said, "you're the very man I wanted to see . . . . About that book of yours . . . you know, *Spoken English* or something . . . I forget the exact name . . . did you—er—go over it carefully before it went to the printers?" So of course I said, "Good heavens, Grey, yes. You don't suppose I'd let them publish anything with my name to it without knowing whether they'd done it properly?"

So then he said:

"Well, look here—er—I don't want to hurt your feelings but, well, to put it bluntly, there are a lot of mistakes in it."

So I said:

"Really? That's interesting. Can you mention one off-hand?"

So he said:

"Well, you've got two in one sentence."

I guessed what was coming as a matter of fact. But I kept quiet about it. I pretended to think he was referring to some misprints I hadn't noticed, you see. So I just said:

"Hm! That's rather serious. I'm sorry about that. I went through it very carefully indeed before it was printed."

So he went on:

"Well, one of the mistakes *may* be a misprint. But the other can't be. You've put a preposition at the end of a sentence. And you put *who* for *whom*. You've put "Who's it by?" on the first page, and a little later you say, "It depends who you're speaking to". Everyone'll see it directly they pick the book up. They'll say, "That's a fine person to learn English from! Why, he can't talk it properly himself. Who does he expect to buy a book like that? And both you and your publishers will be laughed at."

So of course I said:

"Well, if anyone says that to me, I shall just say, 'Well, what's good enough for a Professor of Ancient Languages is good enough for me'."

He said, "Professor of Ancient Languages? Who do you mean?" So of course I said: "You. You've just made the very mistakes you accuse me of. First you said, "That's a fine person to learn English from" (that's a preposition at the end of a sentence). Then you went on by saying "Who does he expect to buy a book like that?" (that's *who* instead of *whom*). You said I and my publishers would be laughed at (a preposition at the end of the sentence), and you've just finished by saying "Who do you mean?" (that's another *who* instead of *whom*).

Of course he denied he said so. People like Grey never do admit they talk that way. And of course you can't prove it unless they've been talking into a gramophone. Still, he knew all the time he had said it, so he began to say, "Oh, well, I was only saying what *other people* would say. Very likely they wouldn't speak correctly."

So I said, "You know perfectly well that you —and ninety-nine out of every hundred educated Englishmen—*always* talk like that."

So he said: "You don't know what you're talking about." You see? He'd put a preposition at the end of the sentence again!

Then he saw what he'd done and began correcting himself. Of course I couldn't help laughing, and that put him in a bad temper. He's not spoken to me since.

EXERCISES

I. *Explain why* "whom" *and not* "who" *is used in the following sentences:*

1. I met a boy *whom* you know.
2. Do you know the boy to *whom* I am referring?
3. Yes, I know the boy *whom* you mean.

4. He is the brother of a boy *whom* I taught.
5. There is the man *whom* I wrote the letter to.
6. There is the man from *whom* I got a letter.
7. Those children, *whom* you saw studying grammar, are in my class.
8. The children about *whom* you spoke are learning grammar.
9. The man with *whom* I was talking is the pilot of the plane.
10. The man *whom* I got the information from is the pilot of the plane.

Rewrite these sentences in a "colloquial form".

II. *Put in the correct interrogative or relative pronoun (a) for formal writing, (b) for ordinary informal writing and speech if different from (a), and (c) say whether it is an interrogative or relative pronoun.*

1. — is that boy?
2. That is the boy — won the race.
3. — car is that new one?
4. To — did you give my best hammer?
5. — shall we ask about a new television set?
6. — goes there?
7. I don't know — work this is.
8. — are you looking for? (*of a person*)
9. He is a person — I trust.
10. Solomon was a king to — the Queen of Sheba gave many gifts.
11. With — did Lilian go to Stratford?
12. It was Caesar — Brutus killed in Rome.
13. "— threw that?" said the master angrily.
14. The boy, to — the ruler belonged, got up slowly.
15. "It is always you — make trouble," said the master.

III. *Use the following verbs in sentences:*

1. laugh at
2. laugh about
3. speak of
4. speak to
5. wait for
6. wait at

7. put up with
8. put up
9. talk about
10. talk to
11. look for
12. look at
13. look after
14. remind . . . to
15. remind . . . of
16. call in
17. call out
18. call for
19. pass down
20. pass by

IV. *Put in the correct prepositions:*

1. Lilian and Andrew live — Scotland not far — Inverness.
2. Sir Winston Churchill thinks a preposition is sometimes a good word to end a sentence — .
3. What did you do that —?
4. John Bunyan wrote most — his greatest book, *Pilgrim's Progress*, while he was — prison.
5. Five planes flew low — the field — which the men were working.
6. Come here — once!
7. I am writing — a pen — my hand, and I am sitting — a chair — a table.
8. It is shady — the trees — the river.
9. The army marched — the bridge.
10. Professor Grey was not the sort — man — whom you could argue.
11. He was never wrong — anything.
12. I expect you are tired — the sentences — this exercise now.

Composition Exercises

1. Tell or write the story of Mr. Priestley and Professor Grey.

2. Tell a story about someone you know who is never wrong.

LESSON 18

Some Strange, but Very Important Verbs. "The Specials" (i)

MR. PRIESTLEY: I wonder if you've noticed in our study of English grammar the strange behaviour of a group of verbs that we might call the "Peculiars" or the "Specials".[1] They are a little band of rebels that insist on going their own way, refusing to be influenced by the behaviour of all the other verbs. Practically all of them are the verbs most frequently used in the language. You already know them all. There are only twelve of them. One or two of the group are not quite whole-hearted rebels—they are inclined sometimes, as you will see, to go over to the side of the majority—but the others are real out-and-out rebels. Here they all are with the related forms in brackets:

> be (am, is, are, was, were); have (has, had);
> can (could); do (does, did); shall (should);
> will (would); may (might); must; ought;
> need; dare; used to.

[1] Dr. Palmer and some other grammarians call them the Anomalous Finites.

OLAF: In what ways are they different from all the other verbs?

MR. PRIESTLEY: In nine ways.

I. In the first place they form their interrogative simply by inversion, that is by putting the verb before the subject, e.g.

Affirmative	*Interrogative*
She was there.	Was she there?
They can speak English.	Can they speak English?
They ought to finish the work.	Ought they to finish the work?

You can't do that with any of the ordinary verbs. As you know, you must use *do* (*does*, *did*), e.g.

Affirmative	*Interrogative*
He speaks English.	Does he speak English? (NOT "Speaks he English?")
I write quickly.	Do I write quickly? (NOT "Write I quickly?")
He finished his work.	Did he finish his work? (NOT "Finished he his work?")

II. These verbs form the negative differently from all the other verbs. They make their negative merely by adding *not*. In spoken English this is shortened to *n't*. A sure way of recognising these verbs is by this shortened form of *not* (e.g. *isn't*, *haven't*, *don't*, *oughtn't*, etc.). They are the only verbs that combine like that with *not*. Here are examples:

Affirmative	*Negative*
She was there.	She was not (wasn't) there.
They can speak English.	They cannot (can't) speak English.
You ought to finish the work.	You ought not (oughtn't) to finish the work.

The ordinary verbs don't do that. You can't say (though at one time you could) "He speaks not English". You must use *do* and *not*, e.g.

Affirmative	*Negative*
He speaks English.	He does not (doesn't) speak English.
I write quickly.	I do not (don't) write quickly.
He finished his work.	He did not (didn't) finish his work.

III. I have mentioned before[1] those common "question phrases":

> It's time for dinner, *isn't it?*
> You would do that, *wouldn't you?*
> He can speak Russian, *can't he?*

or the other type:

> They mustn't do that, *must they?*
> He can't speak Russian, *can he?*
> He speaks Russian, *doesn't he?*

You notice, you don't say "He speaks Russian, *speaks he?*"

The only verbs that can be used in question phrases are our rebels: *be, have, can, do, shall, will, may, must, need, ought, dare, used to.*

PEDRO: Excuse me, but aren't there two meanings to some of these question phrases according to the tone of voice that you use?

MR. PRIESTLEY: Yes, that's quite true; for example, if

---

[1] Book 1, pp. 222, 232.

I want information or confirmation of an opinion I say the question phrase with a rising intonation like this:

"It's raining, ↗isn't it?" (You see, I'm not quite sure whether it's raining or not and I want confirmation. The answer might be: "No, the rain's stopped now.")

"Your name's Brown, ↗isn't it?" (I am not quite sure that his name is Brown. The answer might be "No, it's Smith.")

"We needn't pay the money, ↗need we?" (Here again I'm doubtful whether I need to pay or not.)

Then there's the other form with a falling intonation. In this case you are not asking for information. The "question" is just a conversational remark.

"It's a nice day, ↘isn't it?"

(I know quite well it's a nice day, and I know I'll get an answer like, "Yes, very nice.")

"Your name's Brown, ↘isn't it?" (and I am sure I'll get an answer like "Yes, it is.")

But whichever meaning I want to express, the only verbs that can be used are: *be, have, can, do, shall, will, may, must, need, ought, dare, used to.*

These verbs are sometimes called **auxiliary** (that is "helping") verbs because they help other verbs to form their different tenses (e.g. He *was* walking. I *shall* go. They *have* written) or moods (e.g. Long *may* she reign) and the passive voice (e.g. The work *is* done by machinery). But *be* and *have* are not always auxiliaries. (See page 175.)

HOB: I can tell you a story with a lot of auxiliaries. Here it is:

THREE CHEERS FOR THE NAVY!

Jack, an old sailor who had spent many years in the Navy, was walking along a country road when he came to a farm-house. The farmer was standing at the door and Jack said, " I have been walking all day looking for work. Will you give me a job ?"

"Have you ever done any farm-work ?" said the farmer.

"No," said Jack. "I have been a sailor all my life, but I will do any job you like to give me."

"All right," said the farmer. "I'll give you a chance. Do you see that flock of sheep scattered over the hillside?"

"Yes," answered Jack.

"Well," said the farmer. "Get them all through that gate and into the yard."

"Right," said Jack. "I'll do that."

About an hour later the farmer went to the yard. Jack was leaning on the gate wiping his forehead.

"Did you get them all in ?" said the farmer.

"Yes," said Jack. The farmer looked and sure enough all the sheep were gathered in the yard and the gate was shut. And then the farmer saw a hare running round among the sheep. The sailor saw what he was looking at.

"Yes," he said, "that little fellow there gave me more trouble than all the rest put together."

EXERCISES

I. *Use the following words and phrases in sentences:*

1. band
2. rebel
3. insist
4. go their own way
5. whole-hearted
6. out-and-out
7. tone
8. confirmation
9. in this case
10. doubtful

II. *Give examples of "special" verbs: (a) forming a negative, (b) forming an interrogative, (c) forming a tense, (d) forming the passive voice, (e) forming the subjunctive.*

III. *Pick out the auxiliaries in Hob's story (there are seventeen in all) and say what work each one is doing.*

IV. *Make the following sentences* (a) *negative*, (b) *interrogative*, (c) *interrogative by adding question phrases expecting the answer,*"*Yes*",(d)*interrogative by adding question phrases expecting the answer,* "*No*".

(e.g. It is raining. (*a*) It isn't raining.
(*b*) Is it raining ?
(*c*) It is raining, isn't it ?
(*d*) It isn't raining, is it ?)

1. These verbs are difficult.
2. My aunt is awake.
3. You saw the ashes in the sand-glass.
4. He ought to change his doctor.
5. The students can speak Italian.
6. Lucille spoke Italian well.
7. The policeman will arrest the thief.
8. He used to eat an apple and some chocolate for lunch.
9. Olaf plays tennis well.
10. He has a new tennis racket.
11. We shall arrange a party for our friends.
12. You must go now.
13. The boys could swim across the Thames.
14. They did it easily.
15. Professor Grey was wrong.
16. I am right.
17. You should polish your shoes every morning.
18. You need to find a better job (*the "to" disappears in* (a) *and* (b)).
19. He caught a fish in the Seine.
20. We may have a swim.
21. You can find your way in the moonlight.
22. It will be warm on the beach.
23. Jock had a large bone.
24. He ought to grow a beard.
25. You have almost finished.

LESSON 19

Hob's Story: "Uncle Theophilus"

(I'm afraid we're rather late in getting into
Mr. Priestley's lesson today; it looks as if it's just
finishing; but we'll listen to the last part of it.)

MR. PRIESTLEY: ... Well, I think that's enough grammar for today, but before we go on to something
else, do you remember, Hob, what an auxiliary
verb is?

HOB: An auxiliary verb? ... an auxiliary? ... No,
I'm sorry I don't know.

MR. PRIESTLEY: But I told you about it only yesterday.

HOB: Yes, I've heard the word—at least I think I
have—but I've completely forgotten all about it.

MR. PRIESTLEY: Oh, Hob, what a memory you've
got!

HOB: Yes, it's terrible, isn't it. But talking about
"memory" reminds me of my Uncle Theophilus.

LUCILLE: What, another uncle?

HOB: Oh yes, and the best of the family. May I tell
them about him, Mr. Priestley?

MR. PRIESTLEY: Well, as I don't suppose you'll ever
know what an auxiliary is, and as this lesson is
really over now, I think you might as well.

HOB: Thank you sir. Well, my Uncle Theophilus (we
always call him Theo) is the uncle with the real

brains. You would like him, Mr. Priestley—he could tell you at once what an auxiliary is. He's my oldest uncle, a tall, thin, grey-haired man whose thoughts were always on learning and nothing else. He's quiet and gentle and absent-minded and with about as much sense as a child where money is concerned. Well, he applied for a post in Camford University. It was a very good post and there were hundreds of candidates who applied for it, and about fifteen, including Theo, were asked to go to be interviewed.

Now Camford is a very small town; there is only one hotel in it, and this was so full that they had to put many of the candidates two in a room. Theo was one of these, and the man who shared the room with him was a self-confident fellow called Adams, about twenty years younger than Theo, with a loud voice, and a laugh that you could hear all over the hotel. But he was a clever fellow all the same and had a good post in Iscariot College, Narkover. Well the Dean, that's the head of the department of the University, and the committee interviewed all the candidates; and, as a result of this interview, the number was reduced to two, Uncle Theo and Adams. The committee couldn't decide which of the two to take, so they decided to make their final choice after each candidate had given a public lecture in the college lecture-hall. The subject they had to speak on was—just a moment while I look at

my notebook. Yes, it was "The Civilisation of
the Ancient Sumerians"; and the lecture had to
be given in three days' time.

Well, for three days Uncle Theo never left his
room. He worked day and night at that lecture,
writing it out and memorising it, almost without
eating or sleeping. Adams didn't seem to do any
preparation at all. You could hear his voice and
his laughter in the bar where he had a crowd of
people round him. He came to his room late at
night, asked Uncle Theo how he was getting on
with his lecture, and then told him how he had
spent the evening play-
ing billiards, or at the
theatre or music-hall.
He ate like a horse and
slept like a log; and
Uncle Theo sat up
working at his lecture.

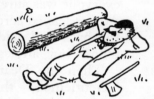

HE SLEPT LIKE A LOG

The day of the lecture arrived. They all went
into the lecture-room and Theo and Adams took
their seats on the platform. And then, Theo discovered, to his horror, that the typewritten copy
of his speech had disappeared! The Dean said
he would call on the candidates in alphabetical
order, Adams first: and, with despair in his
heart, Theo watched Adams calmly take the
stolen speech out of his pocket and read it to the
professors who were gathered to hear it. And
how well he read it! Even Theo had to admit that
he couldn't have read it nearly so eloquently
himself, and when Adams finished there was a

great burst of applause. Adams bowed and smiled, and sat down.

Now it was Theo's turn. But what could he do? He had put everything he knew into that lecture. His mind was too much upset to put the same thoughts in another way. With a burning face he could only repeat, word for word, in a low, dull voice the lecture that Adams had spoken so eloquently. There was hardly any applause when he sat down.

The Dean and the committee went out to decide who the successful candidate was, but everyone was sure what their decision would be. Adams leaned across to Theo and patted him on the back and said, smilingly, "Hard luck, old fellow, but, after all, only one of us could win."

Then the Dean and committee came back. "Gentlemen," the Dean said, "the candidate we have chosen is—Mr. Hobdell." Uncle Theo had won. You could have knocked him down with a feather. The audience were completely taken by surprise, and the Dean continued, "I think I ought to tell you how we arrived at that decision. We were all filled with admiration at the learning and eloquence of Mr. Adams. I was greatly impressed; I didn't think he had it in him. But, you will remember, Mr. Adams *read* his lecture to us. When Mr. Hobdell's turn came, he repeated that speech, word by word from memory, though, of course, he couldn't have seen a line of it before. Now a fine memory is absolutely necessary for this post; and what a memory Mr. Hobdell must have! That is why we decided that Mr. Hobdell was exactly the man we wanted."

As they walked out of the room, the Dean came up to Uncle Theo, who was so confused but so happy that he hardly knew whether he was standing on his head or his heels; and as he shook Theo's hand he said, "Congratulations, Mr. Hobdell! But, my dear fellow, when you are on our staff, you must be more careful and not leave valuable papers lying about!"

MR. PRIESTLEY: Which just shows that Deans (and even teachers of English) are not quite so innocent as some people think they are. Well, Hob, you may not have a memory like your Uncle Theophilus—but you certainly can tell a good story.

EXERCISES

I. *Use the following words and phrases in sentences:*

1. completely	11. share
2. terrible	12. memorise
3. concerned	13. bar
4. apply	14. billiards
5. absent-minded	15. to his horror
6. nothing else	16. eloquently
7. all the same	17. applause
8. interview (verb)	18. word for word
9. final	19. feather
10. candidate	20. valuable

II. *Answer these questions:*

1. What relation was Hob to Theo?
2. How many people applied for the post at Camford?
3. What sort of a man was Uncle Theo?
4. What sort of a man was Adams?
5. How did Uncle Theo spend his time before the lecture?
6. How did Adams spend it?
7. Why did Hob need to look at his notebook while telling this story?
8. Why didn't Adams trouble to do any preparation?
9. Why did Adams say, "Hard luck, old fellow", before they had heard the committee's decision?
10. Do you think any of the committee guessed Adams had stolen the papers? Give a reason for your answer.

III. *Rewrite these sentences, replacing the dashes with one of the following*—some, any, something, someone, anything, anyone:

1. There was hardly — applause for Uncle Theo.
2. Adams didn't seem to do — preparation.
3. Perhaps the Dean guessed — was wrong.
4. — people thought Adams should have the job.
5. Hob didn't know — about auxiliaries.
6. He just remembered he had heard — about them yesterday.
7. — people have bad memories.
8. Are there — cigarettes in the box?
9. No, I'm afraid there aren't — left.
10. — must have smoked them all.
11. I'll go out and get — more.
12. Won't — come with me?
13. — child knows more English grammar than Hob.
14. I don't know — who can tell a story as well as Hob.
15. I want — fresh strawberries; have you — ?
16. Andrew can't have — more apples; I'm keeping — for Lilian.

17. — has borrowed my pen.
18. Is — else coming today?
19. I thought I heard — at the door.
20. I hope there aren't — more of these sentences

IV. *In the following sentences replace the words in brackets by a single word of the same meaning*. All the words are taken from this piece.

1. The (people who applied for the job) all came to Camford.
2. They were all (seen and asked questions) by the committee.
3. Adams didn't seem to do any (work to be ready) for the exam.
4. After the orchestra finished there was great (clapping and cheering).
5. Sir Winston Churchill spoke so (well and with such feeling) that everyone was stirred.
6. The singer (bent his body as a sign of respect) to the audience.
7. The headmaster couldn't (make up his mind) what to do with the boy.
8. I shan't (say again) the lesson on auxiliaries.
9. I made a copy of the speech, and now I'm trying to (get into my memory) the first ten lines.
10. This bracelet is (worth a lot of money).

Composition Exercises

1. Tell or write in your own words the story of the Public Lecture and the committee's decision.
2. "He who laughs last, laughs loudest" (English proverb.) This was true in the case of Uncle Theo. Can you tell another story in which it was true?
3. Have you ever applied for a job? If so, tell or write the story of what happened.

LESSON 20

The "Special" Verbs (ii): Short Answers

MR. PRIESTLEY: In the last grammar lesson I told you something about those peculiar verbs *be*, *have*, *can*, *do*, *shall*, *will*, *may*, *must*, *ought*, *need*, *dare*, *used to*. But that was not nearly the end of the story. Consider for a moment "Short answers". If, for example, I ask someone the question:

Can you speak Russian ?

A full answer would be "Yes, I can speak Russian", or "No, I can't speak Russian." But in almost every case the answer would be in the "short form". *Yes I can* or *No I can't* (or just *Yes* or *No*).

Here are some more examples of "short answers".

Could he answer the question!	No he *couldn't* (= No he couldn't answer the question).
Will he help us?	*No* he *won't* (= No he won't help us).
Are Lucille and Pedro going to the dance to-night?	Lucille *is*, but Pedro *isn't*.
Has she written the letter?	No , she *hasn't*.

Shall I see you at the party?	Yes you *will* (or **No**, you *won't*).
Dare you go there alone?	No, I *daren't*.
Do you speak Russian?	No, I *don't*.
Did they answer the question?	No, they *didn't*.

There's another type of short answer, e.g.

Who was here first, Pedro or Jan!	Jan *was*.
Who can answer that question?	I *can*.
Who wrote this letter?	I *did*.
Who doesn't understand this?	{ I *don't*. / Hob *doesn't*.
Which is the best of these books?	This one *is*.

Again, our short answers may be used to express **agreement** with an opinion, e.g.

I think Jan is working well.	Yes, he *is*.
Olaf has done well in his exams.	Yes, he *has*.
He'll pay the money all right, won't he?	Of course he *will*.
Don't you think Lucille ought to work harder?	{ Certainly I *do*. / Yes, she *ought*.
That window is open.	So it *is*.
I told you the answer yesterday.	So you *did*.
There's a mouse eating the apples.	So there *is*.
You've dropped your handkerchief.	So I *have*.

Or they may express **disagreement.**

It will take you hours to do this work.	No, it *won't*.
That car must have cost a lot of money.	Oh, no, it *didn't*.
He'll pay the money.	Of course he *won't*.
Lucille works hard.	I'm afraid she *doesn't*.
Why didn't you say you knew him!	But I *did*.

Just note which verbs are in the "short answers" (and they are the only verbs that can be used there). They are *be*, *have*, *can*, *do*, *shall*, *will*, *may*, *must*, *need*, *dare*, *used to*. That is Point IV.

"And so . . ."

You may remember a construction that we had before.[1]

You have written a short story	*and so have I.*
Jan has given the right answer	*and so has Frieda.*
Pedro can speak English well	*and so can Olaf.*
John will help	*and so will Margaret.*
Henry must come	*and so must Charles.*
Lucille speaks French	*and so does Pedro.*
Frieda answered the question well	*and so did Jan.*[2]

Notice that you can't say:

"Frieda answered the question well"	and so *answered* Jan.
or "Lucille speaks French"	and so *speaks* Pedro.

The only verbs that can be used for this construction are *be*, *have*, *can*, *do*, *shall*, *will*, *may*, *must*, *need*, *ought*, *dare*, *used to*.

"Neither (nor) . . ."

All those sentences that we have just examined were affirmative ones. With them the construction is "And so . . .". With negative sentences there is a

---

[1] Book II, p. 108.
[2] Notice that in this construction the subject comes *after* the verb and not, as is usual, *before* it.

somewhat different construction: "Neither (nor) has
...". And once again the subject follows the verb,
e.g.

Jan hasn't given the right answer	*neither (nor) has Frieda.*
Pedro can't speak Russian	*neither (nor) can Olaf.*
John won't help	*neither (nor) will Margaret.*
Henry mustn't come	*neither (nor) must Charles.*
Lucille doesn't speak Arabic	*neither (nor) does Hob.*
Frieda didn't go to the dance	*neither (nor) did Jan.*[1]

I suppose I needn't tell you that the only verbs that
can form this construction are *be, have, can, do, shall,
will, may, must, need, ought, dare, used to.*

Just one final point. There is a construction
that combines the "short answer" and the "question
phrase". It is used when we want to express surprise,
or to say something in a rather unpleasant, quarrel-
some way. You will need to listen carefully to get the
right tone of voice. Here are some examples.

"I've left my book at home."	"Oh you have, have you?"
"I can't pay you the money I owe you."	"Oh you can't, can't you?"
"I won't be spoken to like this."	"Oh you won't, won't you?"
"I don't like you."	"Oh you don't, don't you?"
"Hob tore the book."	"Oh he did, did he?"
"Pedro hates English coffee."	"Oh he does, does he?"

[1] In the first half of the sentence the verb is in the negative form
hasn't, can't, won't, etc. In the second half the verb is in the affirmative
form *has, can, will,* etc., but it is, of course, made negative by the word
neither (nor).

EXERCISES

I. *Give the full answer and then the short answers,*
(a) *affirmative*, (b) *negative, to the following:*

1. Can he speak Russian?
2. Will they come to dinner tomorrow?
3. Ought I to answer the letter?
4. Is Hob asleep again?
5. Do you go to the pictures often?
6. Did you hear what he said?
7. Have you spoken to him about it?
8. Shall I see you tomorrow? (*Be careful with "shall".*)
9. Will you be at the party tomorrow?
10. Didn't they finish the work?

II. *Give short answers to the following expressing*
agreement:

1. Jan is a very lucky fellow.
2. He'll come again tomorrow, won't he?
3. Lucille speaks English well.
4. Olaf answered that question correctly.
5. Don't you think he ought to pay the money?
6. You said that before. So — — .
7. It's begun to rain. So — — .
8. That window's open. So — — .

III. *Give short answers to the following expressing*
disagreement:

1. It will be two hours before you get there.
2. That house must have been built before 1940.
3. They built that house before 1940.
4. He'll return the book he borrowed.
5. Your car runs well.
6. Why didn't you tell me so? But — — .
7. Why are you angry with me? But — — .
8. Lord Northwood has a lot of money. Oh, no, — — .

IV. *Give first the full answer, then the short answer to each of the following questions. The first word of the answer is given:*

1. Who is the better swimmer, Jan or Hob? Jan . . .
2. Who can open this door? I . . .
3. Who will help me to move this table? Olaf . . .
4. Who did that exercise correctly? Frieda . . .
5. Who didn't do the exercise correctly? Hob . . .
6. Who gets up every morning at seven o'clock?

(*Give two answers to No. 6, (1) beginning "I . . .",
(2) beginning "Olaf . . .".*)

V. *Use the constructions "and so . . ." and "neither (nor) . . ." with the following:*

1. I will write to you.
2. Jan plays football well.
3. Olaf didn't go to the cinema.
4. Lucille won't be at the dance tonight.
5. Olaf doesn't dance well.
6. Frieda needn't do the work.
7. Pedro must do the work.
8. Jan did the work.
9. Olaf likes walking and swimming.
10. Lucille doesn't like English cooking.

VI. *Add question phrases expressing surprise, or anger:*

1. I don't like this exercise.
2. Hob hasn't done his homework.
3. You mustn't open that box.
4. I'm very fond of chocolate.
5. I'd rather have chocolates than cake.
6. I hate sausages.
7. We've three dogs in our house.
8. The students want a holiday tomorrow.
9. I thought you would give us one.
10. I told him what you said.

TROUBLE IN THE HOME (see p. 152)

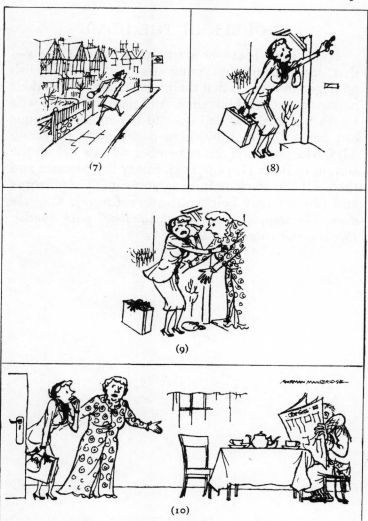

(Reproduced by permission of the Proprietors of "Punch")

TROUBLE IN THE HOME

There is an idea—how true it is, I don't know—
that one reason why young wives, at least English
ones, get annoyed is that their husbands *will* read their
newspaper at breakfast time. And then the young wife
leaves her husband and goes to her mother to pour
out her sorrows. Now, here is the story of young
Mrs. Macpherson (you remember we saw her on the
station in Book II, page 114). Study the pictures and
then tell the story as fully as you can. These words
and phrases may help you: *angry* (*anger*), *bang the
door*, *bus stop*, *dressing-gown*, *handbag*, *pack* (verb),
slippers, *suit-case*.

LESSON 21

The "Special" Verbs (iii)
The Emphatic Form   Position of Adverbs
Third Person Singular

MR. PRIESTLEY: I have already mentioned six peculi-
arities of the "special" verbs, but there are still
three others. Sometimes we want to make a
statement more emphatic. We do it by stressing
one of the verbs in the sentence strongly, like
·this:

> My sister *will* be pleased to see you.
> We *have* enjoyed your visit.
> You *can* sing beautifully.
> Oh, I *should* like a holiday in Switzerland.
> I *do* enjoy good music.

If we want to emphasise the negative element, we
stress the word *not* or *never*, e.g.

> I did *not* steal the book.
> They will *never* agree to that.
> You ought *not* to do that.

But the only verbs that can take this stress for
affirmative emphasis are the "specials"; and the
only time that you can stress the *not* or *never* is
when these words come immediately after one
of the specials.

We sometimes want to be emphatic because we are feeling rather angry, we feel we have been wrongly accused and we want to justify ourselves, e.g.

"Why don't you work hard?"	"But I *do* work hard."
"Why didn't she give him the book?"	"But she *did* give him the book."
"Why won't they keep their promise?"	"But they *will* keep their promise."
"Why haven't you tidied your room?"	"But I *have* tidied my room."

You have noticed, no doubt, which are the verbs that again take the stress.

OLAF: But suppose you stress one of the other verbs. You could do it, couldn't you?

MR. PRIESTLEY: You could, but it would give a quite different meaning. For example, if instead of saying:

"But she *did* give him the book", you said
'But she *gave* him the book"

your sentence would now suggest:

She didn't *lend* him the book, or *sell* him the book, nor did he *steal* it; she *gave* it to him. You are separating that action from all other actions; you are not clearing up all doubt as to whether she gave it or not. Do you see the difference?

OLAF: Oh yes, that's quite clear. In the sentence: "But she *did* give him the book", the only point to be settled is "did she give him the book, or didn't she?" In "But she *gave* him the book", we know he has the book. The only point to be settled is how did he get it; did he buy it, borrow it, or get it as a gift?

MR. PRIESTLEY: Excellent, Olaf. I couldn't have made it clearer myself. That, then, is peculiarity number seven.

The position of certain adverbs

One of your difficulties, I know, concerns the position within a sentence of certain adverbs, the adverbs *never*, *always*, *often*, *sometimes*, *generally*, *almost*, *nearly*, *quite*, etc.

A general rule is that they come just before the verb, e.g.

> I *always* sleep with my windows open.
> He *never* pays the money he owes.
> She *often* hears good music.
> I *nearly* missed my train.
> He *quite* forgot that he had a lesson at 10 o'clock.

But the "specials", as you might expect, are different. They are generally *followed* by these adverbs, e.g.

> I **have** *always* slept with my windows open.
> He **will** *never* pay the money he owes.
> She **can** *often* hear good music.
> He **had** *nearly* missed his train.
> I **had** *quite* forgotten that I had a lesson.

That is the eighth peculiarity.

PEDRO: But don't they sometimes come *before* the verb? I think I have seen cases when they do.

MR. PRIESTLEY: Yes, they can. But then they have a special emphatic use, e.g.

"Jan seems very busy today."	"He always *is* busy."
"You are early this morning."	"I generally *am* early."
"Pedro answered that question."	"He usually *can* answer the question."
"Hob hasn't passed the examination."	"He never *will* pass it."

Third Person Singular

Finally, here's one other little point of difference. The third person singular, present tense of all the ordinary verbs is formed by adding "s" or "es" to the 1st person, e.g.

I write	he writes
I speak	he speaks
I wash	he washes
I go	he goes

But look at the specials; they don't add s or es:

I am	he is
I have	he has
I do	he does[1]
I shall/will	he shall/will
I can	he can
I may	he may
I must	he must
I ought	he ought
I need	he need
I dare	he dare

[1] *Do* is like the ordinary verbs so far as spelling is concerned.

There they are, rebels to the last. An interesting group of verbs, aren't they?

Here is a little conversation to illustrate the emphatic forms:

"Susan's Kitchen"

LUCILLE, PEDRO. (*They have been doing some shopping.*)

LUCILLE: Oh, I *am* tired.

PEDRO: What about having a coffee?

LUCILLE: You *are* a clever boy. That's just what I want. But I will *not* go to that horrid little café in Park Street.

PEDRO: There's a new café, just opened in the High Street. It looks very nice; here it is, "Susan's Kitchen".

LUCILLE (*entering*): Oh, this *is* nice. I *do* like those bright-coloured table-cloths and these fresh flowers on the table.

PEDRO: Look who is bringing in the coffee-cups. It's Susan, who used to be with Mrs. Priestley.

(*Susan comes to their table*)

SUSAN: Good afternoon, sir. Good afternoon, Miss Lucille. It *is* nice of you to come to our café.

LUCILLE: Susan, you *have* furnished your café prettily. You must have worked very hard.

SUSAN: Oh yes, Miss Lucille, we *did* work hard. Joe, my husband, fitted up the shelves and the electric lighting. But, of course, you haven't met my husband, Joe.

LUCILLE: But I *have* met him. He works at Bradshaw's garage where I keep my car. He's the best mechanic they have.

SUSAN: Thank you. Joe *will* be pleased when I tell him; and, though I say it myself, he *is* a good mechanic.

And now I want you to try our coffee. I think you'll like it.

(*She brings them a cup of coffee*)

There you are.

PEDRO: Will you give me the bill, Susan?

SUSAN: There's no bill. I want to give you this.

PEDRO: Oh, no, Susan, I *must* pay you.

SUSAN: No, not this time. But I *do* hope you'll come again often.

LUCILLE: Oh, yes, Susan, we *shall*. I *do* like this coffee, don't you, Pedro?

PEDRO: I certainly *do*. It *has* been nice to see you again. Good-bye, Susan.

SUSAN: Good-bye, and thank you.

LUCILLE: Good-bye, Susan, and give my regards to Joe.

SUSAN: I will, Miss Lucille. Joe *will* be pleased that you have been here.

EXERCISES

I. *Say the following sentences, stressing one of the verbs in each in order to make the sentences emphatic:*

1. Mrs. Priestley can play the piano well.
2. Andrew is a big boy for his age.
3. I shall be glad to be home again.
4. We were sorry you had to go so early.
5. You will try to come again, won't you?
6. I must get this work done before Friday.

II. *Write the following sentences in the Emphatic Form:*

1. Hob likes cake.
2. He enjoyed the ones he ate at the party.
3. I like the cakes that Mrs. Priestley bakes.
4. We had a good swim this afternoon.
5. You bought a lot of chocolate.
6. Andrew runs fast.
7. The wind blew hard when we were at sea.
8. You brought a lot of clothes with you.
9. Jan came here quickly.
10. Jan comes here quickly.
11. Hob drank a lot of lemonade.
12. They took a long time to come here.
13. Those shoes I bought wore well.
14. He promised he would write and he wrote.
15. It froze hard last night.
16. You told me to see the picture at the cinema and I saw it.
17. He asked me to teach him French and I taught him.
18. You did these exercises well.

III. *Give an emphatic answer to the following:*

1. Why don't you come by bus?
2. Why hasn't he written to his brother?

3. Why won't he sign the paper?
4. Why isn't he willing to come here?
5. Why aren't you going to the dance?

IV. *Explain the difference between:*

"But I *did write* to him," and
"But I *wrote* to him."

V. *Read or write the following sentences, putting in the given adverb:*

1. Olaf makes a mistake (sometimes).
2. Olaf has made a mistake (sometimes).
3. I listen to the radio (often).
4. Hob does his work well (never).
5. I have listened to the radio (often).
6. Hob has done his work well (never).
7. I come here by bus (usually).
8. I can come here by bus (usually).
9. Mr. Priestley is busy (always).
10. Mr. Priestley *is* busy (always).

VI. *Rewrite the following sentences, putting the adverbs (in brackets) in the correct position:*

1. I get up at seven o'clock (always).
2. He has done this before (never).
3. Jan and Frieda are early for their class (generally). Hob comes late (usually).
4. Mary comes to our house (often). Margaret has come with her (often).
5. I think (sometimes) that Hob will learn grammar (never).
6. We have finished our work (nearly); I forgot (nearly) it had to be done by six o'clock.
7. It is not easy (always) to do something that you have done before (never).

8. I have seen deer in these woods (never) but my father says he saw one (often) when he was a boy.
9. We go for a holiday (sometimes) in May and we get good weather (usually).
10. We go for a holiday in August (generally) and we have had good weather (nearly always). (*Remember "had" is sometimes a full verb.*)

Composition Exercises

1. Tell or write the story of what happened when Pedro and Lucille wanted a cup of coffee.
2. Describe your idea of a perfect restaurant.

LESSON 22

Olaf Writes a Letter from Oxford (i)

Sept. 3*rd* 19—

(Olaf wrote this letter home. The first part consisted of purely personal matters, so that has been left out. He continues:)

... but I want to tell you about the pleasantest time I have had since I came to England. John, Mr. Priestley's son, invited me to Oxford for a week-end. He's an undergraduate there. He loves Oxford and seems to know all about it. He met me at the station and took me to the "guest room" at his college where I was to stay during my visit. Then we went to his rooms. They are on one side of the "Quad" (quadrangle) up a little narrow stairway with the number of his room and his name, "47 J. Priestley", painted neatly on the wall in white letters. He has a big study, with a desk, bookcase (with lots of books in it), armchairs, cupboards, reading-lamp, and some pleasant drawings of Oxford on the walls. It looked very comfortable, I must say. He has also a bedroom and a tiny kitchen where he can make tea or coffee if he has friends in his rooms. He took wine-glasses from the cupboard and we had a glass of sherry and then went out to see Oxford. Nearly all the students are on vacation just now but we saw a few of them about.

They were wearing black gowns and queer-looking caps, not at all like the caps that our students at Upsala or Lund wear. Some of the gowns looked very old and even rather ragged, and I asked John if these students were very poor and couldn't afford new gowns. He laughed and said that undergraduates, especially those who had just come up, tried to get old, torn-looking gowns so that people would think they had been in Oxford for years. One student passed us, looking rather worried and wearing a black suit under his gown, a white collar and a white bow-tie. John said they had to wear that dress when they were taking an examination, and that unhappy-looking student was either going to or coming from the examination room.

We went into some of the colleges, through the quadrangle and gardens and into the dining-halls and chapels. The colleges are where the students live and they all have dinner together in the big dining-halls.

Most of the halls are wonderful, especially the hall of Christ Church. This is the biggest, at least as far as buildings are concerned, and, perhaps, the most magnificent of the colleges. Its chapel is the Cathedral of Oxford; this is a much older building than the college and had originally been an abbey, the Abbey of St. Frideswide. St. Frideswide is a Saxon saint who died in A.D. 750 and is buried under the floor of the Cathedral.

The college was founded by Cardinal Wolsey in the 16th century. His hat and his chair are there in the college, but before Wolsey could finish the college he fell from power and died in disgrace and the building was completed by King Henry VIII. All round the hall are portraits of great men who have been members of the college: Wolsey himself, Sir Philip Sidney, William Penn (who founded Pennsylvania), John Wesley, John Locke, Ruskin, Sir Robert Peel, Gladstone, Sir Anthony Eden (Christ Church gave England five Prime Ministers in a single century), and a great many other famous people. These men are merely from *one* college—and there are twenty-six other colleges. So there are many other great names connected with Oxford: Shelley, Dr. Johnson, Sir Christopher Wren, Dr. Arnold and his son (the poet Matthew Arnold), Cecil Rhodes, Gibbon, and dozens of others. I should think nearly every great man in England must have been at Oxford, though John admitted that a few had been at Cambridge. One of the portraits in Christ Church that interested me very much was that of Charles Dodgson, better known as "Lewis Carroll", the writer of the most delightful of all children's books, *Alice in Wonderland*. *Alice* belongs to Oxford, for it was told to the little daughter of Liddell, Dean of Christ Church, during an excursion up the river to Godstow, and I think it is characteristic of the odd things you meet with in Oxford that it was written, not by a typical " children's author ", but by a lecturer in mathematics at Oxford. There is a story that Queen Victoria was so charmed with *Alice in Wonderland* that she gave orders that the next book by this writer should be sent to her. In due course it arrived, and was: *The Condensation of Determinants, a new and brief method of computing Arithmetical Values*.

*　　　*　　　*　　　*

While we were talking, a scholarly-looking man in a cap and gown walked past and smiled at John. As he walked away I said: " Surely he's not an undergraduate."

JOHN: No, that's my tutor.

OLAF: What is a tutor?

JOHN: The Tutorial System is one of the ways in which Oxford and Cambridge differ from all the other English universities. Every student has a tutor and as soon as you come to Oxford one of the first things you do is to go and see your tutor. He, more or less, plans your work, suggests the books you should read and sets work for you to do, for example an essay to write. Each week you go to him in his rooms, perhaps with two or three other students, and he discusses with you the work that you have done, criticises in detail your essay and sets you the next week's work.

OLAF: Does the tutor also give lectures?

JOHN: Yes, he may.

OLAF: But aren't lectures given by the professors?

JOHN: Yes, though professors don't give a great many lectures. They are often appointed not so much to do teaching work as to carry on research in their particular subjects.

OLAF: Can you go to any lecture you like, no matter whether it is by a tutor or professor of your college or not?

JOHN: Yes. Lectures are organised not by the colleges but by the university, and so any member of the university may attend, for all students are members of a college and of the university. The result is that where you get a famous professor, like, say, Lord David Cecil, who lectures in English Literature, you will often find that his lecture-room is crowded; a dull professor may have only a handful of students.

OLAF: You said that lectures were "organised by the university". Where is the university?

JOHN: It must seem rather strange to you but there isn't really any university at Oxford as there is, for example, at Manchester or Bristol or Edinburgh. Oxford (like Cambridge) is a collection of colleges, each self-governing and independent. "The University" is merely an administrative body that organises lectures, arranges examinations, gives degrees, etc. The colleges are the real living Oxford and each has its own character and individuality. For example, most of the men at Queen's College come from the North of England, those at Jesus College from Wales. Brasenose has a high reputation for its rugger, Magdalen for its rowing men. But remember that there are students of all kinds in each college; I mean you don't get all science students at one college, all law students at another. Every college has its arts men and its science men, its medical students and its engineers. Every student, of course, follows his own course of study, but he gains a lot from living among those who represent all other branches.

OLAF: I saw in the porch of one college some notices about "Societies"; there seemed to be quite a lot of societies.

JOHN: There are dozens of them: dramatic societies, language clubs, philosophy societies, rowing, boxing, political clubs of all colours, cinema clubs—clubs, in fact, for almost every activity under the sun. Each society arranges for a leading expert in his subject to come and talk to its members. So in term time you get a regular stream of politicians, musicians, poets, painters, film-producers and so on. In a way I think we probably get more out of talking and listening at these clubs and societies than from any other side of university life. The best-known society, I suppose, is the Union, a debating club—a sort of training ground for our future statesmen. The next time you come to Oxford you must come in term time and I'll take you to one of the debates.

You'll hear some attempts—not always very successful—by young speakers to be witty. But you'll hear, too, some first-class debating; and if you look round the walls of the Union at the photographs there, you'll see what a number of our greatest statesmen were once "President of the Oxford Union".

OLAF: There's another tutor, I suppose, that man in the cap and gown with those two men in bowler hats behind him.

BOWLER HAT

JOHN: No, he's a proctor. And the two men behind him are "bull-dogs". The proctor's job is to keep discipline, to see that students aren't out after midnight, or aren't driving a car without having first received permission from the proctor.

OLAF: What punishment can the proctor give?

JOHN: Students can be fined a sum of money, or, for a very serious offence, they can be expelled.

OLAF: And the "bull-dogs", what are they for?

JOHN: They are to catch the student if he tries to run away before his name can be taken.

OLAF: By the way, what are you studying? It's medicine, isn't it? You're going to be a doctor.

JOHN: As a matter of fact, I'm not. That was the idea when I came here, but my interest has always been in language learning and language teaching and so I changed from medicine to modern languages. I'm in my last year now.

OLAF: What do you want to do when you leave Oxford?

JOHN: What I should like more than anything else would be to start a school in Oxford for teaching English to foreign students. And if I could get some Olafs and Jans and Friedas there, I should be very happy.

OLAF: I think they'd be very happy, too, to study English in Oxford. Well, I wish you luck.

JOHN: Thanks, Olaf. But let's walk on again; you've hardly seen any of the colleges yet.

(*Continued in Lesson* 24)

*　　　*　　　*　　　*

EXERCISES

I. *Use the following words and phrases in sentences:*

1. undergraduate	6. afford	11. portrait
2. sherry	7. originally	12. connected with
3. queer-looking	8. in disgrace	13. in due course
4. personal	9. power	14. merely
5. ragged	10. it is character- istic of	15. criticise

16. in detail	21. activity
17. appoint	22. expert
18. research	23. politician
19. organise	24. club
20. gain	25. offence

II. *Answer these questions:*

1. What Oxford lecturer wrote a famous book for children?
2. What was the name of the book?
3. What do undergraduates wear for examinations?
4. Why do some undergraduates prefer to buy a ragged gown?
5. What does a tutor do?

6. How many colleges are there at Oxford?
7. Which is the best-known society?
8. What is the job of a proctor?
9. Why does he have two "bull-dogs" with him?
10. What does John wish to do when he goes down from Oxford?

III. *What is the difference between the words or phrases in each of the following pairs? Use each in sentences of your own.*

1. an Oxford college; Oxford University.
2. a guest; a host.
3. a quadrangle; a triangle.
4. a book-case; a book-shelf.
5. a chair; an arm-chair.
6. statesmen; statement.
7. he smiled at John; he laughed at John.
8. a tie; a bow-tie.
9. a chapel; a church.
10. he fined the student; he found the student.
11. John admitted . . .; John permitted . . .
12. a portrait; a picture.
13. a picture of Oxford; a photograph of Oxford.
14. a box; boxing.
15. owning; owing.

IV. *Give questions to which the following statements might be the answer. The question should be concerned with the words in italics.*

1. *John, Mr. Priestley's son*, invited Olaf to Oxford.
2. He met Olaf *at the station*.
3. He has *a study, a bedroom and a kitchen*.
4. They are not like the *caps* that our students wear at Upsala.
5. They wore these old gowns *so that people would think they had been at Oxford for years*.

6. We went *through the quad* to the dining-hall.
7. He saw Wolsey's *hat and chair* at Christ Church.
8. The college was not finished by Wolsey *because he fell from power.*
9. Wolsey, Penn, Ruskin and Gladstone were some of *the great men who have been members of the college.*
10. There are *twenty-six other colleges.*
11. *Lewis Carroll* wrote "Alice in Wonderland".
12. He wrote *children's books and books on mathematics.*
13. *She gave orders* that the next book by Lewis Carroll should be sent to her.
14. *The Tutorial System* is one of the things in which Oxford and Cambridge differ from other English universities.
15. You go to your tutor *every week.*
16. The tutor *discusses your work.*
17. Magdalen has a high reputation *for its rowing men.*
18. The "bull-dogs" are *to catch the student if he tries to run away.*
19. *I should like to start a school for teaching English.*
20. I should like to start a school for teaching English *in Oxford.*

V. The following is half a conversation between two undergraduates. Gordon has just entered his friend's rooms. *Can you put in what John's replies might have been?*

GORDON: Hullo, John. I just came round to see if you were making coffee.

JOHN: —————

GORDON: Oh, thanks.

JOHN: —————

GORDON: Yes, two lumps. Oh, I see you're in the middle of an essay.

JOHN: —————

GORDON: You won't get much sleep tonight then. Nine o'clock is early for a tutorial.

JOHN: —————

GORDON: Mine's at twelve o'clock on Thursdays.

JOHN: —————

GORDON: Yes, though my tutor does talk rather a lot. It makes me late for lunch.

JOHN: —————

GORDON: You're right. I'm not often late when there's anything to eat or drink.

VI. *Put the adjectives and adverbs in brackets into the Comparative or the Superlative e.g.* This hall is (small) than the hall of Christ Church—smaller.

1. This exercise is (easy) than the last.
2. I think Christ Church is (magnificent) than St. John's.
3. However, the gardens of St. John's are (beautiful) of all.
4. The students hope that the gowns look (old) than they are.
5. I think Hob is the (lazy) of the students.
6. Tom ran fast, Dick ran (fast), but Harry ran (fast).
7. John's room looks (comfortable) than Gordon's.
8. Lewis Carroll's writing for children was (good) than his teaching of Maths.
9. Frieda is (lovely) than I thought.
10. The Union is Oxford's (famous) society.
11. (Many) of the men at Queen's College come from the North.
12. That is the (bad) film I have ever seen.
13. A bus is (slow) than a train.
14. A young man sometimes wishes he were (old) than he is.
15. A young woman sometimes would like to be (young) than she is.

Composition Exercises

1. Describe John Priestley's rooms.

2. The undergraduate that Olaf passed looked "rather worried". He was about to take an examination. Can you describe in three or four sentences your feelings before an examination?

LESSON 23

The "Specials" Again (iv): To Be. Can

MR. PRIESTLEY: As I told you, most of the "special" verbs are the most frequently used verbs in the language. At one time, six hundred to a thousand years ago, English was an inflected language, as Polish, Czech, German, Spanish and many other languages still are today. But in modern English practically all those inflections have disappeared. A regular verb, e.g. *walk*, has only four forms:

walk, walks, walked, walking.

An irregular verb may have five forms, e.g.

speak, speaks, spoke, spoken, speaking.

The corresponding Spanish verbs have fifty-nine. The work that the inflected forms used to do is now done by two or three of the "specials". The verb *to be*, for example, is used with a present participle to form the continuous tense, e.g. He *is walking*; she *was speaking*. Or it is used with a past participle to form the passive voice, e.g.

He *was asked* to sign his name.
You *are invited* to the birthday party.

These uses you have, of course, already met.

But there are one or two interesting constructions or usages with the verb *to be* that you might note. Here is one: "When *is* the wedding *to be*" (="When is the wedding going to take place.")

Here's another construction: " I *am* to have tea with Betty this afternoon." Here are some other examples and idiomatic uses of the verb *to be*:

> My sister and her husband Jim *were* to come to see us this week-end, but the arrangement *is off*. She *is* to let me know if they can come next week.
>
> I looked for Hob's homework but, as usual, *it is* nowhere *to be seen*.
>
> That firm *is all out* to make money, honestly or dishonestly; they *are up to no good*, and if they are not careful they will find they *are up against* the police.

And I think you'll hear another one in Hob's reply to my question: "What do you think of a holiday tomorrow, Hob ? "

HOB: I *am all for it !*

MR. PRIESTLEY: Just one final point. Some of the "specials" are used with *do*.[1] The verb *to be* never is, except with the imperative. *Do* is occasionally used in the positive imperative. *Do not* (*don't*) is always used in the negative imperative, e.g.

> *Do be* careful what you are doing, Hob. You nearly knocked that table over.
>
> *Don't be* late tomorrow; and *don't be* surprised if I tell you there's lots more to learn about these "special" verbs.

[1] e.g. *have, need, dare* (see pp. 196, 235, 248).

Can (Could)

Here is another of the "special" verbs, *can*. It has some peculiar features that I have already mentioned[1] but I want to look at it more fully now. *Can* (past tense *could*) has two main uses:

(1) To express ability, i.e. it has the meaning, *know how to*, e.g.

> Pedro *can* speak French.
> Jan *could* play football well when he was quite young.

(2) To express permission, e.g.

> You *can* go now.
> Father said we *could* go to the theatre.

PEDRO: Excuse me, but wouldn't it be better to say "You *may* go now" or "Father said we *might* go to the theatre"?

MR. PRIESTLEY: In theory it would, and some writers of grammar books advise you to use *may* to express permission and *can* only for ability. But English people and American people in ordinary conversation often use *can* in these circumstances.

HOB: I remember I once said to Aunt Eliza, "Can I smoke in your house?" She replied, "You probably *can* but you certainly *may* not."

LUCILLE: Has *can* any other parts besides *could*?

MR. PRIESTLEY: No. It has no infinitive,[2] no imperative, no participles.

---

[1] *Essential English*, Book I, p. 64.
[2] The verb *to can* has a quite different meaning, i.e. to put meat, fish, fruit or vegetables in tins or cans.

FRIEDA: How do you get over the difficulty of the missing parts? Suppose you want the future tense? You can't say "I shall can".

MR. PRIESTLEY: We use "be able". The form "be able" can generally be used instead of *can*, e.g.

> "I *can* do the work" or "I *am able* to do the work."
> "I *could* do the work" or "I *was able* to do the work.'

For the Future Tense we say:

> "I *shall be able* to do the work."

For the Present Perfect:

> "I *have been able* to do the work."

For the Infinitive:

> "I hope *to be able* to do the work."

Could, besides being the past tense, is also used for the conditional, e.g.

> "If you tried, you *could* do that work."
> "I would help you if I *could*."
> Even if he had been here, he *couldn't* have helped you.

PEDRO: Is there any difference in usage between *can* and *be able*? I have a feeling they are not always interchangeable.

MR. PRIESTLEY: You are quite right, Pedro. It is rather a difficult point.

The question only arises in the past tense with *could*. The difference seems to be that for something that you can do because of knowledge or skill (swimming, speaking English, playing football, for example) you can use either *could* or *was able*.

Examples:

A.

I *could* (was able to) swim well when I was only six years old.

Jan hurt his foot and *couldn't* (wasn't able to) play football.

The door was locked and I *couldn't* (wasn't able to) open it.

B.

But we use *was able* and not *could* if we want to express the meanings: "managed to do something" or "succeeded in doing something".

You will see that usage in these sentences:

1. He worked very hard, and *was able* to pass his examination.
2. We had a holiday yesterday and so *were able* to go to the seaside.
3. "I wonder why Jane hasn't come here." "She may not *have been able* to get away from the office."

In sentences B it would be wrong to use *could* because "*be able*" in each case means *managed* or *succeeded*

"... he managed to pass (he succeeded in passing) his examination."

"... we succeeded in getting to the seaside."

"... she may not have managed to get away (succeeded in getting away) from the office."

Strangely, enough, if these sentences are negative, *could* may be used, e.g.

"He worked very hard but *couldn't* (or *wasn't able to*) pass his examination."

"We had a holiday yesterday, but *couldn't* (or *weren't able to*) go to the seaside."

"Perhaps Jane *couldn't* (or *wasn't able to*) get away from the office."

Were you able to understand all that, Pedro?

PEDRO: Yes, I think *we were all able* to understand it.

MR. PRIESTLEY: Good. Now just one final word about *could*. We sometimes use *could* as a kind of weaker variety of *can*. We have a feeling that it is perhaps rather more polite, e.g.

"*Could* you tell me the right time, please?"

And sometimes we use *could* to express a gentle doubt:

"I *could* do the job tomorrow but I'd rather put it off till Friday."

"Yes, his story *could* be true but I hardly think it is."

EXERCISES

I. *Make the following sentences passive:*

1. Shakespeare wrote *Hamlet*.
2. Our College Dramatic Society gave the play last year.
3. Jan took the part of Hamlet.
4. They are giving it again this year.
5. Jan will take the part of Hamlet again.

II. *Replace the words in italics with a construction using some form of* to be. *The constructions required are all in Lesson 23.*

1. *It is arranged that we meet* at five o'clock.
2. When *will* the party *take place*?
3. Jan *does all he can* to pass his examinations.

4. *We had planned* to go to Switzerland last year, but we couldn't go.
5. Today we *face* great difficulties.
6. I support the idea, *whole-heartedly*.

III. Hob wants you to explain this joke of his:
"The Americans grow a lot of fruit. *They eat what they can, and can what they can't.*"

IV. *Replace* can *or* could *in each of the following sentences by the correct form of* to be able:

1. Jan can speak English.
2. I can swim.
3. Hob can't do this exercise.
4. I could swim when I was six years old.
5. He couldn't speak English before he came to England.
6. They can all understand this lesson.
7. They could all understand this lesson.
8. I can tell you Henry's address.
9. I can't tell you Henry's address.
10. He can't tell you Henry's address.
11. We couldn't remember Henry's address.

V. *Say the following in the* future *tense, adding the words in brackets:*

1. I can speak English (after I have had some lessons).
2. I can play football (when my foot is better).
3. Jan can play football (when his foot is better).
4. Olaf can speak English better (after he has had more lessons).
5. We can do this exercise (now we have had it explained).
6. The students can do this exercise (now they have had it explained).
7. Frieda can cook well (when she has had more practice).

8. Hob can't do this work (until he tries harder).
9. I can read a lot of books (when my holidays come).
10. You can see the house (when you get to the top of this hill).

VI. *In which of these sentences can* the words in italics *be replaced by* could?

1. I *was able* to drive a car when I was sixteen.
2. The night was clear and we *were able* to see the stars.
3. After a lot of hard work I *was able* to pass the examinations two years ago.
4. The aeroplane was damaged but the pilot *was able to* bring it safely to land.
5. I *was able* to finish the work by ten o'clock.
6. When I was a boy I *was able* to write with my left hand as easily as with my right hand.
7. *Were you able* to do things with your left hand as easily as with your right hand?
8. After hard fighting the soldiers *were able* to drive the enemy out of the town.
9. The firemen *were able to* put the fire out before it destroyed the house.
10. After I had studied the lesson I *was able to* do the exercise correctly.

LESSON 24

Olaf's Letter from Oxford (ii)

. . . There were so many beautiful and interesting things to see that I hardly know what to pick out as the most beautiful. Perhaps it is Magdalen Tower— I'm sending you a photograph of it. Don't you think it is lovely ? Someone described it as " Sight music that is frozen ". Every year at sunrise on May morning (so John told me, and he got up to see it) the choir of Magdalen gather on the top of the tower to sing a Latin

MAGDALEN TOWER, OXFORD

hymn. The custom goes back to the first days of the tower, at the end of the 15th century, and has gone on ever since. Oxford is full of curious old customs like that. For example, Queen's College was founded in 1341 by Robert de Eglesfield. He must have been a man with a lively imagination for he ordered the college to be governed by a head of the college and twelve Fellows (in memory of Christ and the Twelve Disciples), and he said that on New Year's Day each year, the bursar (the man who is in charge of the money matters of the college) should present each Fellow with a needle and thread of coloured silk saying, "Take this and be thrifty". The needle and thread was a pun on his name, Eglesfield. (The French *aiguille* = needle; *fil* = thread.) With the same idea the shield of the college shows three golden eagles on a red field ("eagles-field"). That was 600 years ago. And still, though Eglesfield's buildings were replaced in the 17th century by the present college, every New Year's Day the bursar presents each Fellow with a needle and thread and says, "Take this and be thrifty." In that same college, too, every Christmas Day a roast boar's head is carried, with great ceremony, to the high table where the dons sit. The story of this custom goes back to the early years of the 16th century and celebrates the fight between a student of the college and a wild boar on the hills near the college. The student killed the boar by thrusting down its throat a copy of Aristotle that he happened to be reading at the time, saying as he did so, "Graecum est" (That's Greek!). As John said, "You can believe the story if you like."

As you walk through Oxford you seem to be living in history, so many things call up events and figures of the past. Here Queen Elizabeth I listened to Shakespeare's plays in a college hall, and made jokes with the professors—in Latin and Greek! In Pembroke College you can see Dr. Johnson's blue and white tea-pot (it holds about two quarts, for Johnson was a great tea-drinker and on one of his visits to Oxford his host poured out for him eighteen cups of tea!). In Oxford, Charles I held his Court at Christ Church while the colleges melted down all their silver dishes to help his cause during the Civil War, and his Queen Henrietta and her ladies walked in the gardens of St. John's (there are two fine statues by le Sueur[1] of Charles and Henrietta in the Quad there). Here, Roger Bacon laid the foundations of experimental science, not in the 18th but in the 13th century; here, every night you can hear the sound of "Great Tom", the big bell in Tom Tower, the tower that Wren designed for Christ Church. Every night at five minutes past nine the bell is rung 101 times in memory of the 101 students in Christ Church in Henry VIII's time. In the medieval library of Merton College you can see all the chained books and the old benches just as they were in the 13th century. These reminders of the past are everywhere.

John and I walked along St. Giles, one of the most beautiful streets in Oxford. It is not, like most of the Oxford streets, narrow and winding between colleges, but very wide with magnificent trees all the way along

[1] Le Sueur made the statue of Charles I that stands in Whitehall, London, said to be the finest statue in London.

it. And there, outside Balliol College, is a monument very like the "Cross" at Charing Cross[1] in London. I asked John what it was. He said, "It's the Martyrs' Memorial. Bishop Latimer and Ridley and Cranmer were condemned to death at Oxford in 1555[2] for their religious beliefs and were burned at the stake in this place. As the fire was being lighted Latimer said, 'Be of good comfort Master Ridley and play the man. We shall this day light such a candle, by God's Grace, in England as I trust shall never be put out.'"

MARTYRS' MEMORIAL

*   *   *   *

As I said, Oxford is not only beauty in stone, it is history in stone. John pointed out two church towers. "That is the tower of St. Martin's and that of St. Mary's. In the 14th century there were constant quarrels between the men of Oxford and the students of the University, or, as they said, between the 'town' and the 'gown', and on St. Scholastica's Day,[3] 1354, a quarrel broke out in an inn between some students and some townsmen. Others joined in, and soon the bells of St. Martin's Church (the church of the townsmen) were ringing to gather the townsmen together. The Chancellor (that is the head of the University) tried to stop the fighting but he was shot

[1] The Charing Cross is one of a series that Edward I had built at every place where the body of his wife Eleanor (who had died in Scotland) rested on its last journey to Westminster.

[2] Cranmer in 1556.   [3] February 10th.

G

at and had to retreat. So the bells of St. Mary's (the church of the students) were rung to collect the students together, and they shot at the townsmen with bows and arrows. Two thousand people from the countryside round Oxford came into the city to help the townsmen; colleges were attacked and the battle went on for three days. The King, Edward III, was at Woodstock, about eight miles from Oxford, and he ordered the Chancellor of the University and the Mayor of Oxford to appear before him. He decided that the townspeople had been in the wrong and ordered the Mayor and the chief citizens of Oxford to attend the Church of St. Mary's every St. Scholastica's Day for a service in memory of the students who had been killed in the fighting, and to pay an offering of forty pence. And for nearly 500 years,[1] every St. Scholastica's Day, the Mayor and chief citizens of Oxford went to St. Mary's and paid the forty pence."

The morning after this chat with John, I was very forcibly reminded of another old Oxford tradition. I was awakened at five o'clock in the morning by a terrible noise in St. Giles outside the college, the noise of hundreds of people. Half-awake, I thought for a moment that another St. Scholastica's riot had broken out, and quickly dressed and went outside to see what was happening. I discovered that it was St. Giles' Fair. This has taken place at the beginning of September ever since the 12th century. The whole appearance of St. Giles was quite changed. Preparations for the fair mustn't begin before 5 a.m. At five

[1] The custom was ended in 1826.

o'clock the entrances to St. Giles are closed to traffic. I looked out, and there, waiting to rush in, was a stream of carts, cars, wagons, roundabouts, swings, coconut-stalls, strong men, and "all the fun of the fair". It's all very noisy and jolly and you'd probably think it was rather silly—but it's great fun while it lasts.

It's all these contrasts in Oxford that make the place so fascinating. Oxford doesn't live only in the past; you feel there is a sense of continuity all through its history. To go from Magdalen Bridge, where the lovely Tower stands like a guardian of the city, through Radcliffe Square, the heart of the University, past the great Bodleian Library (to which a copy of every book published in Great Britain has to be sent) and on to the fine new science buildings of the

Clarendon Laboratories, is to pass through streets where the Middle Ages, the 18th century and the modern world rub shoulders. Here, men have expressed in stone the finest culture of their periods. Norman, Gothic, Renaissance, Classic, Modern are all there in friendly rivalry, each beautiful thing adding something to the contrasting beautiful thing that is its neighbour. I felt very strongly this mingling of old and new when we visited New College, which, in spite of its name, is one of the oldest colleges.[1] Here, against a background of Gothic stonework, is the gigantic statue of Lazarus, carved by Epstein only a few years ago. And in New College I saw one of the most moving things I have seen in Oxford, moving because it seemed to me to express so well the noble, generous spirit of Oxford. It was a war-memorial that said:

> In memory of the men of this College who, coming from a foreign land, entered into the inheritance of this place and, returning, fought and died for their country in the war 1914–1919.

> Prinz Wolrad-Friedrich zu Waldeck-Pyrmont
> Freiherr Wilhelm von Sell: Erwin Beit von Speyer.

The men to whom that memorial was raised were Germans who had fought against England.

The beauty of these buildings and the peace of the colleges and the loveliness of the gardens like St. John's and Worcester, these are the things I shall never forget. I'm afraid my letter has wandered on

---

[1] It was started in 1380. The oldest colleges are Merton, University College and Balliol, all between A.D. 1250 and 1300.

at great length, but I can't finish without—as my friend Hob would say—telling you a story that I had from John. I happened to say to him as we walked through one of the gardens, "I wonder how they get these lovely lawns." John said, "That's what an American visitor asked one of the gardeners here. He said he'd like to have a lawn like that in his big house in America. 'Oh, it's quite easy,' said the gardener, 'you just roll them and cut them and roll them and cut them. That's all.' 'And how long do you do that?' said the American.

'Oh,' said the gardener, 'for about five hundred years'."

There's lots more I'd like to tell you about Oxford, but that must wait until I see you again.

Love to you all,

OLAF.

EXERCISES

I. *Use the following words and phrases in sentences:*

1. photograph	9. medieval	17. fair (noun)
2. imagination	10. reminder of the past	18. contrast
3. income	11. monument	19. fascinating
4. expenditure	12. quarrel	20. publish
5. thread	13. retreat	21. culture
6. needle	14. tradition	22. gigantic
7. celebrate	15. half-awake	23. noble
8. event	16. riot	24. at great length

II. *Answer these questions:*

1. Why do some undergraduates get up early on May 1st?
2. Why does Olaf say that Robert de Eglesfield must have had a "lively imagination"?
3. What work does the bursar of a college do?
4. Do you believe the story of the boar and Aristotle? Give a reason for your answer.
5. What famous man (he made the first great English dictionary) came from Pembroke College?
6. Why does Great Tom sound 101 times every night?
7. What reminded Olaf of Charing Cross?
8. What does a quarrel between "town" and "gown" mean?
9. Which road is closed to traffic early in September? Why?
10. What is the difference between St. Giles and many other Oxford streets?

III. *Put* since, for *or* till *in the blank spaces:*

1. The custom has continued — 1254.
2. That must wait — I see you again.
3. The singing of the Latin hymn has gone on — more than 350 years.
4. Preparations for the fair can't be made — five o'clock in the morning.
5. — nearly 500 years the money was paid.
6. I didn't get to bed — midnight.
7. I haven't been to Norway — six years.
8. Don't move — I say so.
9. I've been waiting here — four o'clock.
10. He has been teaching — twenty-nine years.
11. What have you been doing — yesterday?
12. "You must roll the lawn — about five hundred years," said the old gardener.
13. I've been reading this book — three hours.
14. I haven't looked at this photograph — years.
15. It has been raining — yesterday afternoon.

IV. *Turn the following sentences into questions* (a) *asking for information*, (b) *expecting an answer "Yes"*, (c) *expecting an answer "No"*, e.g. John is up at Oxford. (*a*) Is John up at Oxford ? (*b*) John is up at Oxford, isn't he ? (*c*) John isn't up at Oxford, is he ?

1. That is Magdalen tower.
2. Cranmer was burnt to death at the stake.
3. Olaf thought the students' gowns were ragged.
4. He wants to go to Oxford again.
5. You have done sentences like this in Book II.
6. Mr. Wiggins fell off the ladder.
7. Hob can't understand Latin.
8. A party of Americans is visiting Oxford.
9. The lawns of St. John's garden are beautiful.
10. You would enjoy a visit to Oxford.
11. Adams drinks far too much.
12. Olaf ought to play more tennis.
13. Wolsey founded Christ Church.
14. You shouldn't have done that.
15. This exercise is finished now.

Composition Exercises

1. Tell or write the story of three of Oxford's curious old customs.

2. Find out more about three of the following: Samuel Johnson, Sir Christopher Wren, Shelley, Cecil Rhodes, and Sir Anthony Eden. Write a little about them (100–150 words).

3. Have you ever been to Oxford ? If so, say what you enjoyed about it most. If not, say what you would like to see most.

TEST PAPER No. 2

I. *Put the verb in brackets in the correct tense:*

1. He should be there by now, if he (go) straight home.
2. You should (hold) the ladder steady, and then I shouldn't have fallen.
3. I shouldn't think of asking you to (wash) the dishes.
4. I shouldn't (like) Mr. Priestley to see this exercise.
5. The train should be here by now, but it (be not).
6. The train would be here by now, if it (be not) foggy.
7. They should have mended your watch by now, unless the spring (have) broken.
8. He said he would sit there as long as he (want) to.
9. Would you mind (help) me with this bag?
10. If he (do) that again, I should have knocked him down.

II. *In which of the sentences of No. 1 can you replace* should *by* ought to *? Rewrite these sentences using* ought to.

III. *Use the following phrases in sentences showing that you understand their meaning:*

1. take it easy
2. till late at night
3. for help
4. nothing I should like better
5. worth waiting for
6. do without
7. hurt . . . feelings
8. as a matter of fact
9. out-and-out
10. in due course

IV. *Rewrite these sentences in the negative. Use the short form of verb where possible.*

1. I was very happy to see him.
2. He hit the ball hard.
3. I will give a tip to the waitress.
4. You must leave the paper on the ground.
5. He ought to wash his neck.
6. That Italian speaks English well.
7. You need a haircut.
8. England lost the football match.
9. I shall go to the pictures after this Test Paper.
10. You have enough money, haven't you?

V. *Put the adverbs in their correct places in these sentences:*

1. He brings home an evening paper. (usually)
2. He has brought home an evening paper. (sometimes)
3. "You are up early." "I am up early." (always)
4. He can hear the news from Moscow on his wireless. (often)
5. Why do you remember that I don't take sugar in my tea? (never)

VI. *Complete the following sentences in your own words:*

1. Hob's story could be true, but . . .
2. I felt very strongly that . . .
3. It has been nice . . .
4. It will be two hours before . . .
5. . . . , won't he?
6. There was hardly any applause . . .
7. I don't suppose . . .
8. You mustn't . . .
9. A dozen times a day . . .
10. Whatever you say, I . . .

VII. *Replace* can *and* could *in these sentences by the correct form of* to be able:

1. Can you hear me properly?
2. I can't hear what you're saying.
3. He could play the violin beautifully.
4. You can do this lesson easily.
5. That family can all sing well.
6. He couldn't remember my name.
7. I can drive a car.
8. We couldn't finish the job yesterday.
9. Couldn't he come today?
10. No, I'm afraid he couldn't.

VIII. The following is half a conversation between Hob and Olaf in Mr. Priestley's room. *Can you put in what Olaf might have said?*

HOB: I say, Olaf, there's still five minutes before Mr. Priestley comes. Can you help me with last night's exercise?

OLAF: ————

HOB: Oh, thanks.

OLAF: ————

HOB: I've got it here.

OLAF: (*looking in Hob's book*): ————

HOB: I expect you're looking in the wrong place. I know, I'll start again. You just say the answers and I'll write them down.

OLAF: ————

HOB: Oh, I don't think he'll mind. After all, he wants us to get them right.

OLAF: ————

HOB: The trouble was there was a good T.V. programme last night, and I didn't get much time for them.

OLAF: ————

HOB: Yes, I can hear him, too. Oh, dear, I don't think he'll be very pleased.

IX.   *Composition Exercises*

Write about 200 words on one of the following:

   (*a*) Oxford.
   (*b*) A character study of a friend.
   (*c*) Which do you prefer, the cinema or the theatre ?

X. *Read the following passage carefully and answer the questions below:*

As he crept up this rise in the ground, he knew that he could not go much further. His body was weak, but worse than that, his will to keep going, his will to live, had almost died away. It seemed now to Alan like a horrible dream in which he was a helpless actor. Three days without food or water had almost broken his spirit. He dragged himself slowly across the burning sand to the top of the hill and with tired eyes looked beyond.

At first he saw nothing but the sight he had seen for days. Then, away to his right, his eyes fixed on a dull spot of green. Trees. That meant water. That meant life. With a great effort he rose to his feet and with unsteady but determined steps he moved on.

(1) *Give another word or phrase with similar meaning to that in which these words and phrases are used in the passage: (a) crept, (b) almost, (c) for days, (d) unsteady, (e) determined.*
(2) *Why did Alan's journey seem to him like a dream ?*
(3) *In what sort of country was Alan travelling ?*
(4) *What brought back to him "his will to live" ?*
(5) *Suggest in about eighty words what might have happened before this extract, explaining why Alan was in such a difficult situation.*

LESSON 25

The Special Verbs (v): Have

MR. PRIESTLEY: I told you in an earlier talk that some of the "special" verbs are sometimes conjugated with *do*. One of these is *have*, and students (even really advanced ones) often find difficulties here. Do we say "Has he?" or "Does he have?", "She hadn't" or "She didn't have"? What do you think?

OLAF: I think I have heard both forms, but I'm not sure when I must use the one and when I must use the other.

MR. PRIESTLEY: You are quite right, both forms are used. Look at these sentences:

> *Has*[1] *your sister* brown eyes or blue eyes?
> Has[1] *Switzerland* a good climate?
> This room *hasn't*[1] enough windows in it.
> I *haven't*[1] a lot of time to spare.

HOB: As I say: "I haven't much money, but I do see life."

MR. PRIESTLEY: Quite so. Those interrogatives were formed by inversion, and the negative simply by adding *not* ('*n't*). But look at these sentences with *have*. These, too, are all correct:

[1] Very often in conversation we use *got* also; e.g. "*Has* your sister *got* blue eyes", "This room *hasn't got* enough windows", etc.

196

"Did you have a letter from home this morning?"

"I didn't have much breakfast this morning."

"What time *did you have* it?" "The usual time, we *don't* usually *have* it until about nine o'clock."

"Did you have tea or coffee?"

"I don't have much difficulty with English Grammar."

"Did you have a good time at the dance last night?"

PEDRO: I think that in the first group of sentences— the ones that made their interrogative by inversion—the meaning of *have* was, roughly, *possess*. But in the second group of sentences, the ones that are conjugated with *do*, the word *have* does not mean *possess*.

"I *haven't* much money" means "I don't *possess* much money", but "I didn't have much breakfast" means "I didn't *eat* much breakfast."

JAN: Oh yes. "Did you *have* coffee or tea?" means "Did you *drink* coffee or tea?"

FRIEDA: And "I didn't *have* a letter from home" means "I didn't *get* (or receive) a letter".

OLAF: And "I don't *have* much difficulty with grammar" means "I don't *experience* much difficulty".

LUCILLE: And "I didn't *have* a good time at the dance" means "I didn't *experience* (or enjoy) a good time". (Though, as a matter of fact, I *did have* a good time last night.)

HOB: All I know is that I *have* a headache with all this grammar and I *hadn't* a headache when I came here.

FRIEDA: Do you often have a headache when you have to discuss grammar?

HOB: Yes, I do!

JAN: Just a moment. Your rule doesn't seem to apply here, Pedro. Hob said, "I have a headache . . . I hadn't a headache"—that's the negative without *do*.

PEDRO: Quite correct because *have* there means *possess*.

JAN: Yes, but Frieda said "*Do* you often *have* a headache?" which means, roughly, "Do you often *possess* a headache?" She was using *do* with *have* even though *have* meant *possess*.

MR. PRIESTLEY: And Frieda's sentence was quite correct. Pedro's rule covers some cases but there are one or two other points to be considered.

1. When the "possession" is a *permanent* thing; as, for example, in the case of your sister's brown eyes, we don't use *do* with *have*.

2. When we are speaking of something that is regular or habitual—like Hob's headache over grammar—we use *do* with *have*. So "*Do* you often *have* headaches?", i.e. are they regular and habitual, is correct.

3. We do not use *do* when we are speaking of one particular occasion. You can compare:

> *Do* you often have headaches? (habitual).
> *Have you* a headache *now*? (particular occasion).[1]

---

[1] American usage is different. In America *have* is generally conjugated with *do*. So you will hear: "Do you have a wife?" (*American*). "Have you (got) a wife?" (*English*). "*Does* he *have* any children?" (*American*). "Has he (got) any children?" (*English*).

Causative Use of "Have"

I must also point out the "causative" use of *have*; that is where we use *have* to show that we cause something to be done, e.g.

> We have just *had* our house painted (= caused our house to be painted).
>
> I've just *had* my hair cut; when did you *have* yours done?

The verb *get* is also used with the same meaning in this construction: e.g. I *got* my hair cut today; where do you generally *get* yours done?

Then there is a similar construction where instead of *causing* something you *suffer* something, e.g.

> I *had* (or *got*) my pocket picked (i.e. something stolen from my pocket) yesterday.
>
> He *had* (or *got*) his arm *broken* playing football. *Did* he? (Note the usage with *do*.)
>
> You won't *have* (or *get*) your house burgled as easily as I did if you keep a good dog.

Have to (= must)

Finally there is another use of *have*. It is used to express compulsion, obligation or necessity.

> You *have to*[1] work hard nowadays to make a living.
>
> My car wouldn't start this morning so I *had to* (I'd got to) walk to the office.
>
> We *had to* (we'd got to) answer all the questions in the examination.
>
> You *haven't* (*got*) *to go* home yet, have you?
>
> Will he *have to* do the work all over again?

[1] Or more often in colloquial English, "You have (you've) *got* to work hard . . ."

As you can see from these examples, the usual construction for *have to* (= must) is without *do*.

But occasionally, if we are speaking about something that is regular or habitual, we use the *do* construction.

> A. *Do* you *have* to write exercises every day?
> B. No, we *don't have* to write them every day but I like to write them as often as I can.

And now, I don't think there is much that you don't know about *have*. I think we *had better* stop. You'll *have to* think about what I've said—and I hope you *haven't* all *got* a headache!

EXERCISES

I. *Make these sentences interrogative:*

1. Her brother has curly hair.
2. A triangle has three sides.
3. You had eggs and bacon for breakfast this morning.
4. He had a letter by the evening post.
5. They have a lesson every day.
6. He has a lot of money.
7. They have a lot of trouble with their car.
8. Lucille had an enjoyable time at the dance.
9. Frieda has a bad cold.
10. She often has a cold in winter.

II. *Make these sentences negative:*

1. I have a dark blue suit.
2. A triangle has four sides.
3. I had coffee for breakfast this morning.
4. I had some letters by morning post. (*Be careful with "some".*)

5. They have lunch before twelve o'clock.
6. We have a lesson every day.
7. Mr. Brown has a lot of money.
8. We had a very comfortable journey to Scotland.
9. That country has a very good climate.
10. I have some cigarettes in my cigarette-case.

III. *In the following sentences use* got *instead of just* have, *e.g.* Has he any complaints ? Has he got any complaints ?

1. The butcher hasn't any change.
2. Mr. Wiggins has an Austin car.
3. Have you your books with you?
4. She has a new refrigerator.
5. I've some lovely flowers in my garden.
6. Have you everything you want?
7. I thought you had a new hat.
8. By this time tomorrow I shall have his reply.
9. He hadn't a job when last I saw him.
10. How much money has Uncle Albert?

IV. *Rewrite these sentences using some part of* have *or* get *with a past participle, e.g.*

The tailor made a new suit for me last week.
I *had* a new suit *made* for me last week.

1. Someone cleaned my shoes for me.
2. Painters painted my house last week.
3. One of my teeth was taken out this morning.
4. Someone must chop this wood for us.
5. We must ask someone to mend the car.
6. Someone picked Pedro's pocket at the football match.
7. It's time your hair was cut.
8. Jan broke his leg playing football.
9. This knife won't cut. We must ask someone to sharpen it.
10. His house was burgled while he was away on holiday.

LESSON 26

The "Special" Verbs (vi): Do

MR. PRIESTLEY: We've talked a lot about *do*, and rightly, for it is perhaps the hardest-worked verb in the language. You see it is both a "full" verb and a "special". You see its work as a full verb in such sentences as:

> He *does* his work well.
> What *were* you *doing* this morning?
> What *does he do* for a living? He doesn't *do* anything.

When it is a "full" verb, it is conjugated with *do* as you can see in that last example.

We have already seen much of its work as a "special" where it is used to form the negative and interrogative of all verbs except the "specials" (and sometimes even with them). It is used to show emphasis, as in Hob's remark on p. 196.

> "I haven't much money, but I *do* see life."

and for short answers to avoid repeating the verb.

> Do you understand that? Yes, I *do*.
> Do you like grammar, Hob? No, I *don't*.
> You know that as well as *I do*.

Again, it is used for question phrases with all the verbs that aren't "specials":

> You understand that, *don't you?*
> You didn't come by bus, *did you?*

Finally it is used in the constructions:

> I like swimming, and *so does Olaf.*
> Olaf doesn't like flying; neither *does* Hob.

HOB: And when we meet someone we say, "How *do* you *do* ?"

MR. PRIESTLEY: And I think *that will do* for grammar today.

*   *   *   *

FRIEDA: I received a quite exciting letter this morning, Mr. Priestley. It was from Mr. and Mrs. Evans. They are old friends of my father's and they live at Capel Curig, a little village in North Wales. They stayed last Christmas with us at my home in Switzerland, and now they have invited Jan and me (they met Jan last Christmas; you remember he came to spend Christmas at our house) to have a holiday in August at their house in Wales. I have always wanted to go to Wales; Mr. Evans talked so much about it, and now I'm going to get the chance of seeing it. Isn't it lovely ?

MR. PRIESTLEY: That's splendid news, Frieda. I'm sure you will both enjoy it; it's a fascinating country, both for its scenery, which is some of the loveliest in the world, and for its people and its traditions.

PEDRO: I envy you your holiday there, Frieda; I wish I were going there, too. You'll probably come back speaking Welsh.

HOB: But don't the Welsh people speak English?

MR. PRIESTLEY: Most of them do, but that's not their native language.

FRIEDA: Mr. Evans speaks English as well as Mr. Priestley does, but Welsh is his mother tongue.

OLAF: How does it happen, Mr. Priestley, that the people there speak Welsh? After all, it is near England, it's not separated from it by the sea, and I suppose it has been part of the British Isles for hundreds of years.

MR. PRIESTLEY: What Olaf says is quite true, but it is too big a subject to go into just now; but, one day, I'll give you a lesson on "Why the Welsh speak Welsh" and, incidentally, "Why the English speak English," for, at one time, the inhabitants of this island didn't speak English.

JAN: I should like that very much, sir. I'm sure I don't need to tell you how much I am looking forward to this holiday in Wales. While I am there I want to write a "diary" of the things that I have seen and heard.

FRIEDA: And I'll write down some of the stories that I'm sure Mr. Evans will tell us and we'll send you the "diary" and the stories, or bring them with us when we return so that you can all read them.

MR. PRIESTLEY: That is an excellent idea, Frieda. We shall look forward very much to reading them.

EXERCISES

I. *Make three sentences using* do (a) *as a full verb*, (b) *as a "special" verb.*

II. *In what constructions is* do *used as a special verb?*

III. *Put in the correct form of "do".*

1. You are — very well.
2. — you — that exercise on your own?
3. How — you —?
4. You know Mr. Jones, — you?
5. You must — as well as you can.
6. I — like eggs and bacon.
7. What — he — in the evenings?
8. He swam the English Channel, — he?
9. Jan enjoys a game of football, and so — Olaf.
10. — you speak Dutch? No, I —.
11. Hob — — anything, unless he has to.
12. Lucille — like brandy, and neither — Olaf or Jan.

IV. *Answer the following:*

What does the baker
　　　　carpenter
　　　　engineer ⎫do?
　　　　cook
　　　　dressmaker

Composition Exercise

There is an English proverb, "When in Rome do as the Romans do." What do you think this means? Is it good advice for a traveller?

Wales

0 10 20
Scale in miles

Beaumaris
Anglesey
Conway
Llanfair P.G.
Caernarvon
Llanberis
Menai Straits
Snowdon
Beddgelert
Criccieth
Harlech

CARDIGAN

BAY

Cardigan
Fishguard
St. David's
Swansea
Caerleon
Cardiff

🏰 denotes Castle

LESSON 27

Frieda Writes a Letter from Wales

Capel Curig,
N. Wales.

Dear Mr. Priestley,

Well, here we are in Wales; and what a lovely country it is. I was very excited when we crossed from England into Wales. The map shows a boundary between England and Wales, but there was no "frontier", no Customs officers, no armed guard. But you know you are in Wales all right, you soon hear Welsh being spoken, you see Welsh names on the sign-posts and you see them on the railway stations. One of these is:

Llanfairpwllgwyngyllgogerychwyrndro-
bwllllantysiliogogogoch[1]

I know Hob won't believe this, but it's true, and I will bring him a picture postcard of the station to prove it.

I can't tell you about all our journey; it would take a book not just a letter, but I should like to tell you of a trip we made yesterday in Mr. Evans' car round

[1] The station is in Anglesey. The name means: "The church of St. Mary in a wood of hazel trees near a rapid whirlpool and near St. Tysilio's cave not far from a red cave". The town is generally known as "Llanfair P.G."

some of North Wales. We went through lovely countryside, with great mountains, some of them beautiful and green and wooded, others bare and wild. There were gentle, fertile valleys with little farmhouses or cottages sheltering on the slopes of the mountains, and quiet lakes and rivers winding down or, in places, dashing down to the coast, which is only twenty or thirty miles away; in places the mountains run right down into the sea.

We went to Snowdon, in fact we went up Snowdon, the highest mountain in England and Wales. The mountain is dark and wild-looking: but my home is among the mountains of Switzerland, and though Snowdon is impressive, well, it isn't Mont Blanc or the Jungfrau. We actually went right to the top of Snowdon *in a train*. (I daren't tell this to my Swiss mountaineering friends!) It happened like this. We had just gone through the town of Llanberis at the foot of the mountain, and there was a little station and in it was a little engine and train, just like the toy trains and station that my young brother has at home. So we got in. The carriages held fifteen or sixteen people and, with a lot of smoke and steam, the toy train moved out and puffed its way round and round and up the mountain.

For a time we had fine, extensive views, and then, all at once we entered a cloud. The whole view was blotted out. A thick grey mist was all around us, in the carriage (for it was quite open without any windows) and in our eyes and throats. And wasn't it cold! I sat close to Jan to try to keep warm. Suddenly, after about half an hour, we came through the cloud and into the sunlight. The train came to a stop in another little station and we were at the top of Snowdon. The clouds were breaking everywhere below us and through the gaps we had a wonderful view for miles, right across the Menai Straits to the Isle of Anglesey. Behind us we could see the enormous shadow of the two peaks of Snowdon, the one on which we stood, the highest one, and the slightly smaller peak beside it. Mr. Evans said something in Welsh. It was poetry and it sounded beautiful though I didn't understand a word of it. I asked him about it. He said it was from the poem *The Day of Judgment* by the Welsh poet Goronwy Owen. He wrote the lines down for me and I'm sending them so that Lucille and Olaf and the rest will know what Welsh looks like:

> "Ail i'r ar ael Eryre,
> Cyfartal hoewal â hi"

and it means: "(on that day) the head of Snowdon shall be levelled with the ground, and the circling waters shall murmur around it."

But I'm no good at describing things or expressing ideas; I must leave that to Jan; he's much cleverer than I am, as you know. What I like doing is telling a story and Mr. Evans told us two that I want to tell you. He told us the first one as we came into the little town of Beddgelert that lies in a lovely valley about ten or twelve miles from Snowdon. We got out of the car and he took us a short walk along the side of a stream until we came to what looked like a little grave-stone. And this is the story he told us:

In the 13th century, Llewellyn, Prince of North

Wales, had a palace here. He had a faithful dog, Gelert, that went with him everywhere and that he was very fond of. But one day the Prince went out hunting, and he told Gelert to stay at home and guard the Prince's baby son. Gelert obediently lay down by the cradle of the baby, and Llewellyn went away. When he returned in the evening, Gelert came out joyfully to meet him, and the Prince was horrified to see that the baby's cradle was overturned, the bed-clothes and floor were covered with blood and there was blood round Gelert's mouth. The baby was nowhere to be seen. The Prince thought the dog had killed the child and wild with rage and fear he drew his sword and thrust it into Gelert's heart. The dying cry of the dog was followed by a child's cry. Llewellyn looked round hastily, and there, under the torn and bloodstained blankets, was his baby son, quite safe. And beside it was the body of a huge wolf that Gelert had killed in defending his master's son.

Llewellyn was so filled with sorrow that it is said he never smiled again. He buried Gelert in this spot; and ever since, the place has been known as Beddgelert, which means "The Grave of Gelert".

*　　　*　　　*　　　*

My other story concerns Caernarvon, where we went on another day. It's a very interesting town, at least 2,000 years old. To the Romans it was Segontium and they built a great fort there. But what over-shadows everything else in Caernarvon is the castle. When Edward I,[1] King of England, was trying to

---

[1] Reigned 1272–1307.

conquer Wales he built a great line of castles—the ruins of which you can still see at Harlech, Criccieth, Beaumaris and Conway—but Caernarvon was the greatest. It's the most magnificent thing of its kind, said Mr. Evans, in Great Britain. If you approach it from the sea, or if you stand outside under its walls, it looks exactly as it must have done when Edward built it to keep the Welsh in subjection, but when we went inside we could see the ruin that 600 years have

CAERNARVON CASTLE

caused. "Look at that little doorway that was the entrance to the dining-hall of the King," said Mr. Evans. "It was so narrow that only one man could enter at a time, so, if the English King was surprised by an attack as he sat at dinner, his archers could kill the attackers one by one, while the King could get away down that little staircase on the other side.

"Now, come up here," he said, "to the top of the Eagle Tower." So we climbed up, and he pointed out stone figures that the builders had cleverly put there. The enemy thought they were soldiers keeping constant watch, but though they shot many an arrow at those watchers they never killed one of them!" Then, with a smile he said, "How Time brings its changes. Edward's city of Caernarvon, where in his time a Welshman daren't set foot without risking death, is now, I should think, the most Welsh city in Wales."

"Yes," said Jan, looking at the stream of visitors below us paying their shillings to the Welsh door-keeper to enter the castle, "in Edward's day the Welsh had to pay money to the English; and now the English have to pay money to the Welsh."

Mr. Evans thought that was a good joke—and so do I. "Listen," he said, "I'll tell you another story. And this is the story he told:

"Edward I had conquered Wales. The two great Welsh leaders, Llewellyn and his brother David, had been killed. But the Welsh people, though they were beaten, were rebellious. They had no great leader, but there were a number of chieftains—most of whom were jealous of one another—and at last three or four of these chieftains came to see Edward, who, with his wife Eleanor, was staying at Caernarvon Castle, to tell him their complaints and to try to get their wrongs put right.

"They wanted, they said, to be ruled not by an English King, but by a Prince of Wales, born in Wales, of royal blood, and not speaking English or French. They wanted a prince whose life was good, and who had not wronged any man—though, owing, as I said, to their jealousy of one another, they couldn't agree who this prince should be. Well, they were certainly asking a lot, but Edward, after a little thought, told them to ask all the chiefs and their followers to come to Caernarvon Castle in a week's time and he would give them what they had asked, a Prince of Wales who fulfilled all their conditions.

"So the next week the great square outside the castle was crowded with excited people, all wonder ing which of their chieftains Edward had chosen."

I'll not finish the story here. Jan thought it would make a good little play, so *he* has written this next piece, which he has called:

The First Prince of Wales

SCENE: *Caernarvon Castle. A crowd of Welshmen, kept back by English soldiers. A group of Welsh chieftains push their way through the crowd and come to the front.*

1ST WELSHMAN: It won't be long now; look, the chiefs are all here.

2ND WELSHMAN (*to English soldier*): And you won't be here long now.

ENGLISH SOLDIER: What do you mean?

2ND WELSHMAN: When we get our Welsh prince, you English soldiers will all be sent back to England.

ENGLISH SOLDIER: There's nothing I'd like better. I'm tired of the sight of your Welsh mountains and your rain and fog.

1ST WELSHMAN: They are lovely mountains, and it is a lovely country.

2ND WELSHMAN: It will be when you English are out of it.

ENGLISH SOLDIER: All right, all right; but give me good old London every time. Stand back there! Stand back! What are you pushing for? You'll see the show all right from there.

*   *   *   *

1ST CHIEFTAIN: I wonder who the new ruler is to be? Of course, you know my mother was a distant relation of Llewellyn.

2ND CHIEFTAIN: Yes, very distant—about as distant as mine to King Arthur. But it's a pity you took all that trouble to learn English. Edward said he would choose a prince who spoke no English. Welsh was always good enough for me.

3RD CHIEFTAIN: If you think I'd ever agree to having either of you for my prince you are very much mistaken; and I have 2,000 men. Once the English go, there is no one in Wales who would be stronger than I. And of course I don't speak any English— well, not very much.

4TH CHIEFTAIN: But Edward said the prince would have wronged no man. I haven't forgotten those fifty sheep of mine that you stole. I'll not have a thief for prince over me.

3RD CHIEFTAIN: Do you call me a thief? ——

2ND CHIEFTAIN: My father's second cousin was descended from Arthur ——

3RD CHIEFTAIN: Two thousand men, I tell you ——

ENGLISH SOLDIER: Stop that noise! Stand back! Stand back! The King!

(EDWARD *steps from a window on to the balcony in front of the castle. Behind him is a knight carefully carrying* EDWARD'S *shield flat in his hands. On the shield is a bundle covered with a blanket. The whole crowd is excited but silent, and waiting for* EDWARD *to speak.*)

EDWARD: Chieftains and people of Wales, you have asked for a prince and I have promised you one to rule over you, of royal birth.

WELSHMEN: Yes, yes.

EDWARD: Born in Wales.

WELSHMEN: Yes.

EDWARD: And not able to speak a word of English.

WELSHMEN: Yes, yes.

EDWARD: And one, moreover, of blameless life, one who has wronged no man by word or deed in all his life. If I give you such a prince to rule over you, will you promise to be ruled by him?

WELSHMEN: We promise.

EDWARD: Then here is your prince. (*He turns to the knight behind, lifts the blanket, and shows a small baby.*) My son, a prince of royal blood, born a week ago in Wales, in Caernarvon Castle; he speaks no word of English, and he has wronged no man alive. Edward, Prince of Wales!

*　　　*　　　*　　　*

"Well," said Mr. Evans, "the chiefs were angry and disappointed, but the Welsh people were pleased, and each chief consoled himself with the thought that, at any rate, no rival chief had been chosen. And from that day to this, the eldest son of the King and Queen of England has always been the Prince of Wales."

It's time I brought this long letter to a close. Jan and I send our kind regards and best wishes to you and Mrs. Priestley and all my friends who are with you.

Yours sincerely,

FRIEDA.

EXERCISES

I. *Use the following words and phrases in sentences:*

1. boundary	6. bare	11. in places
2. frontier	7. shelter	12. actually
3. customs	8. fertile	13. puff
4. sign-posts	9. slopes	14. round and round
5. trip	10. impressive	15. extensive

16. blot out	21. hastily	26. I'm tired of
17. enormous	22. quite safe	27. bundle
18. peak	23. ruins	28. blameless
19. obediently	24. archers	29. console
20. overturn	25. fulfil	30. from that day to this

II. *Answer these questions:*

1. How did Frieda know she was in Wales?
2. What sort of countryside did she see in North Wales?
3. Why was Frieda less impressed by Snowdon than, perhaps, a young English girl would have been?
4. What sort of train took Frieda up the mountain?
5. What could they see at the top?
6. Who was Goronwy Owen?
7. Why did Llewellyn kill Gelert?
8. What is the modern name for Segontium?
9. Why was the doorway to the dining-hall of Caernarvon Castle so narrow?
10. Why did the builders put stone figures at the top of the tower?
11. Which city did Mr. Evans think was the most Welsh?
12. What conditions did the Welsh chieftains want fulfilled by Edward I when he chose a ruler?
13. How did the chiefs like his choice?
14. How did the Welsh people like his choice?
15. What is the title given to the eldest son of the King and Queen of England?

III. *Rewrite the following sentences using* although *instead of* but (*e.g.* The English tried to conquer the Welsh but they remained free.—Although the English tried to conquer them, the Welsh remained free).

1. The Welsh fought bravely, but they were defeated.
2. Jan had never been to Wales before, but he soon felt at home there.

H

3. Wales was a beautiful country, but the English soldier preferred London.
4. The Welsh chiefs were disappointed, but they accepted their new prince.
5. Hob likes to read, but he does not like to write.

IV. *Make the following sentences passive. Leave out, where it is unnecessary, the doer of the action.* (See Book II, Lesson 27.)

1. Mr. Evans took Frieda and Jan to Snowdon.
2. The valleys shelter the little farmhouses.
3. We could see the enormous shadow of Snowdon.
4. Gelert was guarding the prince's son.
5. Blood covered the floor.
6. The prince buried Gelert at this spot.
7. Edward I built a great line of castles.
8. Mr. Evans is pointing out the stone figures.
9. The English are paying money to the Welsh.
10. Edward I had conquered Wales.
11. He told them to come in a week's time.
12. Olaf has written this little play.
13. The soldiers kept back the Welsh crowd.
14. Edward chose a baby to be their ruler.
15. I must now bring this letter to a close.

V. *Express in one word the meaning of each of the following words and phrases.* All the words come from this lesson. You are given the number of letters.

1. a short journey (4)
2. to show that a thing is true (5)
3. the edge of a country next the sea (5)
4. mountain top (4)
5. small river (6)
6. to look after (5)

7. very large (8)
8. a baby's bed (6)
9. to go towards (8)
10. to go into (5)
11. something shot by archers (6)
12. wanting something which another possesses; fearing that another will take what one has, and therefore hating him (7)
13. someone who steals (5)
14. not speaking or making a noise (6)
15. sad at not seeing one's hopes come true (12)
16. stretching for a long way; wide (9)
17. producing much; fruitful (7)
18. having no clothes or covering (4)
19. quickly; in a hurry (7)
20. to protect (7)

Composition Exercises

1. Tell or write the story of Llewellyn and Gelert.
2. Describe the way Frieda climbed Snowdon.
3. Have you ever climbed a mountain ? If so, tell the story.

Or:

"A mountain summit[1] white with snow
Is an attractive sight, I know,
But why not see it *from below*?"

Do you agree with the author of these lines ? What are your views on mountain-climbing ?

[1]Peak.

LESSON 28

The "Special" Verbs (vii): Ought

MR. PRIESTLEY: The next of our "special" verbs is *ought*. It's like the other specials in forming its interrogative by inversion and its negative with *not*, e.g.

> He knows he *ought to* pay the money.
> *Ought* he to pay the money?
> He *ought not* (*oughtn't*) to pay the money, *ought* he?
> You *ought to* be ashamed of yourself.

(1) The general meaning, you see, implies *duty, what is right*. There is no other form of the verb except this one. There are no infinitives, no participles, no preterite, and the third person singular does not end in *s*.

To give the idea of past time we use *ought* (*oughtn't*) *to have* and a past participle, e.g.

> I *ought to have* written that letter yesterday (with the implication "but I didn't write it").
> You *oughtn't to have* gone to the football match, Hob (". . . but you did").
> You *ought to have* done your homework last night ("but you didn't").
> He *ought to have* told me that before ("but he didn't").

(2) There is another meaning of *ought*, i.e. *prob-ability*, e.g.

> If Lucille left home at nine o'clock, she *ought* to be here any minute now.
> There's a fine sunset; it *ought* to be a fine day tomorrow.
> Considering all the work you have done, you *oughtn't to fail* your examination.

(3) The verb *ought* doesn't use *shall* or *will* for its future tense. If we want to express a future idea with *ought* we do it by means of a word or phrase denoting the future, e.g.

> Jan's team *ought* to win the match *tomorrow*.
> Your suit *ought* to be ready *next Thursday*.
> You *ought* to write to her *as soon as you can*.

(4) *Should* can generally be used instead of *ought* and with practically the same meaning.

> If you owe the money you $\begin{Bmatrix} should \\ ought\ to \end{Bmatrix}$ pay it.
>
> Lucille left home at 9 o'clock; she $\begin{Bmatrix} should \\ ought\ to \end{Bmatrix}$ be here any minute now.
>
> You $\begin{Bmatrix} shouldn't \\ oughtn't\ to \end{Bmatrix}$ have spent all that on a dress.

Note: The infinitive after *ought* always has *to*. With *should* the *to* is omitted.

Well, I don't think there's anything else I *ought* to tell you about *ought*.

EXERCISES

I. *Use* ought *instead of* should *in the following:*

1. You should work harder.
2. It's six o'clock, she should be here by this time.
3. You should have done the work instead of going to the cinema.
4. He shouldn't have been late for that important meeting.
5. I suppose I should have been more careful.

II. *Rewrite the following so that they refer to past time:*

1. You ought to get here by nine o'clock.
2. I suppose I ought to pay the money.
3. How much time should I spend on this exercise?
4. Mr. Priestley ought to tell you about this before you do the exercise.
5. You shouldn't leave my book out in the rain.
6. He ought not to speak like that.
7. Why should I do all the work?
8. Ought I to write out this exercise?
9. How much ought I to give him?
10. The wireless shouldn't make that noise.

LESSON 29

Frieda Tells a Story: King Arthur

(*Extract from Frieda's diary.*)

... I asked Mr. Evans today about King Arthur. His name kept coming up, at Snowdon, in his story about Caernarvon and when he told us about the great Roman city that had been discovered after months of digging in Monmouthshire[1] at Caerleon, "that's Camelot, where King Arthur held his Court" he said.

"Was King Arthur a real person, or is it all a story?" I asked.

MR. EVANS: Oh yes; there was a real Arthur, an Arthur who fought the Saxon invader and won a great battle at Mount Badon in A.D. 500. But around this shadowy human figure, fighting among the mountains of Wales or on the wild cliffs of Cornwall (where you can still see, at Tintagel, the ruins of Arthur's castle), has grown up a great collection of romantic stories that run like a brilliant thread through the pattern of English literature from the early Anglo-Saxon and Norman writers, through Chaucer and Malory to Tennyson. These old stories tell us of Arthur's miraculous coming, of how he

---

[1] In Arthur's time Monmouthshire was part of Wales.

became King and gathered together a brave company of knights—the Knights of the Round Table.

FRIEDA: Why was it round? Had that any special meaning?

MR. EVANS: Yes, it was to show that no knight, not even the King himself, was "head of the table"; all were equal and the King was just "first among equals". You can still see the table—a great round piece of wood hanging on one of the inner walls of Winchester Castle. But though 600 places in the British Isles claim some memory of him, he is for ever essentially the hero of Wales, and it's rather significant that the Welshman who became King of England, Henry VII, called his eldest son Arthur. I think Arthur's name is so widespread throughout England, and the Continent, too, because Welsh bards in Norman times and before that, travelled about singing the songs and telling the stories about him. Those stories were gathered together by Sir Thomas Malory[1] and it is from his *Morte d'Arthur* that all the later writers and poets have drawn the materials for their stories and poems.

FRIEDA: Could you tell us one of the stories of Arthur and his Knights.

MR. EVANS: There's hardly anything that a Welshman likes better than telling a story—unless it's listening to one; and I'm a Welshman.

And this is the story he told us:

[1] About 1470.

The Story of Sir Galahad

One day as King Arthur sat in his Court at Caerleon surrounded by the Knights of the Round Table a servant entered and said, "Sir King I have seen a strange sight. As I walked along the bank of the river I saw a great stone, and it floated on the water. There was a sword through the stone and the handle of the sword was thick with precious stones." When they heard this, the King and all the Knights went to see this strange thing. It was just as the servant had said; moreover, when they looked more closely they read the words on the sword: "No one shall draw me out of this stone except the knight at whose side I am to hang. And he must be the best knight in the world." The knights asked Sir Launcelot to draw the sword, for he was known as the best knight in the world. But Sir Launcelot said: "The sword is not for me. I dare not try to take it." Many of the knights tried, but none could draw out the sword. So they returned and took their places again at the Round Table.

No sooner were they seated than the door opened and an old man, dressed in white, entered the hall, followed by a young knight in red armour, by whose side hung an empty sword-sheath.

The old man bowed low to the King and said, "Sir, I bring you a young knight, Sir Galahad; through him Britain shall win great glory; and he shall see the Holy Grail." "The Holy Grail!"

said the knights, their faces full of awe, for the Holy Grail was the cup from which Christ had drunk at the Last Supper. It had been brought to Wales by Joseph of Arimathea, but because of man's sinfulness it had been taken from human sight. None of the knights had seen it, for it could be seen only by the pure in heart, and all of them had sinned.

When the feast was over, the King took Sir Galahad to see the sword in the stone. "I will try to take the sword," said. Sir Galahad, "for, as you see, my sword-sheath is empty." He seized the handle of the sword and drew it easily from the stone and placed it in his sheath. While they were all filled with surprise, a lady came to them, riding on a white horse, and said, "I am sent to bring you word, O King, that great honour will be done to you and all your knights. Today the Holy Grail will appear in your hall." Then she rode away and no one could ask her any further questions.

That evening as each knight sat in his seat round the table there was a noise of thunder, so great that the whole palace seemed to shake, and there came into the hall a great beam of light, brighter than any of them had seen before. The light touched them all, and a sweet scent was in the air. And in the beam was the Holy Grail. But no one could see it except the pure-hearted Sir Galahad. They all sat silent with amazement and awe until Arthur rose and gave thanks to God for the vision that had come to them.

Then Arthur's nephew, Sir Gawain, stood up and said that he would make a vow to go for a year and a day in search of the Holy Grail. Immediately other knights, a hundred and fifty in all, rose up and swore to do the same; and among them was Sir Galahad.

King Arthur was full of sorrow at this. His knights would wander into far-off countries; many of them, he knew, would forget that they were in search of the Holy Grail, and would go on other adventures and never return. Meanwhile, the heathen enemies from whom he had protected his land would come again to conquer him. Turning to Sir Gawain he said, "Nephew, you have done wrong, for by your act I have lost the noblest company of knights that ever brought honour to any country in Christendom; for I know that you knights, whom I have loved as my life, will never again all gather together in this hall." The knights, too, were filled with sorrow, but they could not break their vows.

So the next day, after they had worshipped in the church at Camelot, the knights who had made the vow rode together out of Camelot, and the people wept as they rode away for they felt they would never return.

FRIEDA: And did they ever return?

MR. EVANS: Some of them did; but not Sir Galahad. He wandered for years searching for the Holy Grail. He had many adventures (every one of which would be a separate story). He rescued maidens who had been imprisoned, he was himself imprisoned for a year by an evil king in Sarras in Babylon where Joseph of Arimathea had lived 300 years before teaching the people the true faith. Finally he was freed and he forgave the king who had imprisoned him, and when that king died, Galahad was made king. But though at times he had seen again the light of the Holy Grail, he never saw it in reality. Every morning, early, he used to go into the little church to pray. Then one morning, very early, as he knelt, he saw a man in the dress of a bishop; and the bishop was surrounded by a great band of angels. The bishop said, "Come here, servant of the Lord, and see what you have so long wished to see." And Galahad took the Grail in his trembling hands. "Do you know who I am," said the bishop?" "No," said the knight. "I am Joseph of Arimathea whom God has sent to show you the perfect vision of the Holy Grail." Then Galahad knelt and prayed. As he prayed a hand came from Heaven and took away the Cup. And when, a little later, the people came to the church, they found Sir Galahad dead.

FRIEDA: What a wonderful story! But what happened to King Arthur?

MR. EVANS: Well, though some of the knights returned, the great days of the Round Table were over. While Arthur was fighting his enemies in France, the wicked knight Sir Modred, whom Arthur had left to rule the land while he was away, plotted against the King and gathered together an army to fight against him. Arthur returned and a great battle was fought in the far west of Britain by the sea shore. The traitors were defeated and Modred was killed by Arthur, but only one of Arthur's knights, Sir Bedivere, was left, and Arthur himself was very badly wounded. Then Arthur said to Sir Bedivere, "The end has come. Take my sword Excalibur and throw it into the deep water. Watch what happens and come back and tell me." So Sir Bedivere took the sword and went to the water's edge. But the handle of the sword was thick with precious stones and he couldn't bear to throw it away. So he hid the sword under a tree and came back to the King. "What did you see?" said the King, "and what did you hear?" And Sir Bedivere said, "I saw nothing but the waves and heard nothing but the wind." "That is untrue," said Arthur. "I order you, as a faithful knight, to go again and throw the sword into the sea." Again Sir Bedivere went, and again he was tempted. "It is a sin and a shameful thing," he thought, "to throw away so noble a sword. It should be kept so that people in all future times can see it and be reminded of this great king." So he left the sword under the tree and returned again to the dying Arthur. "What did you hear; what did you see?" said Arthur slowly. And Bedivere said, "Sir, I saw the water washing on the rocks and heard the wind blowing in the trees." "Traitor," said Arthur, "you have betrayed your knighthood and your name. Go again and do as I command. If you fail this time I will rise and kill you with my hands." Then Sir Bedivere went quickly back to the water's edge and took the sword from where he had hidden it and closed his eyes for a moment so that he should not see the handle and the precious stones, and then he threw it with all his might out to sea. But before the sword touched the water, an arm rose out of the sea and caught the sword, raised it three times and then drew it under the water. Bedivere hurried back to the King and told him what he had seen. "Help me down to the water's edge," said Arthur, "but hurry. I have waited too long, my wound has taken cold and I may die." So Bedivere raised the King and took him on his shoulders and brought him gently down the rocks to the water's edge. And as they reached the shore they saw a small ship there, and in it were many noble figures and among them three queens dressed in black with crowns of gold on their heads. "Put me in the ship," said Arthur. So Bedivere gently lifted the King into it and laid him down. Then the most beautiful of the queens knelt beside him, took off his helmet, which was cut through with a sword, and, looking at his pale face, wept and said, "Dear brother, why have you waited so long?" Bedivere cried out, "Oh my lord Arthur, what shall I do now you are taken from me, and all my friends of the Round Table are dead? Where shall I go, alone, among new men, strange faces, other minds?"

"THE SHIP SLOWLY MOVED AWAY"

And Arthur said, "Find comfort in yourself, for I can give you no comfort. My life is ended. The work of the Round Table is done. The old order has changed, giving place to new; but God's will is done in many ways. Pray for my soul; more things are done by prayer than this world dreams of. I am going now to the Valley of Avilion where my wound may be healed." As he spoke, the ship slowly moved away, and Bedivere watched it until it could be seen no more.

"So," said Mr. Evans, "Arthur went away, and, though you can see his grave at Glastonbury, where it says:

'Here lies Arthur, once King, and King to be'
many people believed that he was not dead but
was still living in the happy valley of Avilion
until his country needed him, when he would
come again to free it from its enemies."

EXERCISES

I. *Use the following words and phrases in sentences:*

1. discover	10. float	19. filled with surprise
2. shadowy	11. armour	
3. human	12. handle	20. beam of light
4. cliffs	13. glory	21. scent
5. romantic	14. awe	22. vision
6. miraculous	15. sinfulness	23. vow
7. claim	16. sin (verb)	24. go in search of
8. significant	17. feast	25. rescue
9. material	18. sheath	

II. *Answer these questions:*

1. Was King Arthur a real person?
2. What English writers have written about him?
3. Why was the Round Table round?
4. Was Sir Galahad present when news was brought by a servant about the sword?
5. Why did Sir Launcelot not try to take the sword from the stone?
6. What was the Holy Grail?
7. Why had none of the knights seen the Holy Grail?
8. What did Sir Gawain say after the vision? Why was Arthur full of sorrow at it?
9. Why did Sir Bedivere twice disobey his King's command to throw away the sword?
10. What did some people believe about King Arthur?

III. *Give an opposite of the following words:*

1. wicked	6. float	11. question	16. deep	21. valley
2. dead	7. best	12. remember	17. round	22. old
3. edge	8. empty	13. servant	18. true	23. under
4. early	9. easy	14. enemy	19. slowly	24. nothing
5. sorrow	10. appear	15. against	20. closed	25. future

IV. *Rearrange the order of the words in these sentences so that they make sense:*

1. us told stories many Mr. Evans King Arthur about.
2. Arthur person was a real, it is or story a all only?
3. still can at Tintagel ruins you castle his see the of.
4. a story hardly anything than that there's a Welshman better likes.
5. many knights but the sword of the out draw could none tried.

V. *Complete the following phrases with words of your own.* (All the phrases have come in the last three lessons.)

1. I thought you would like . . .
2. Could you tell us . . .?
3. There's hardly anything I like better than . . .
4. No sooner had I arrived than . . .
5. It's a pity . . .
6. I'm no good at . . .
7. What I like doing is . . .
8. This story concerns . . .
9. I'm tired of . . .
10. If I . . . will you promise . . .?

Composition Exercises

1. Tell the story of Sir Bedivere and the death of Arthur.

2. Tell the story of a legendary (or real) hero of your own country.

*   *   *   *

HOB: The boys and girls at the school my cousin Ted goes to "acted" the story of King Arthur as the teacher read it to them.
Ted is the boy with the sword!

" And then King Arthur knights Galahad by tapping him gently on the head with his sword . . . *gently !* "

LESSON 30

The "Special" Verbs (viii): Need

MR. PRIESTLEY : One of the difficulties with *need* is that there are really two verbs *need*. One is a full verb, the other is a "special".

I. The full verb is quite regular:

> I need, he needs, I needed, I have needed, I am needing, etc.,

Examples:

> I *need* a new suit [1]; this one is very old.
> I am glad you have had your hair cut; it *needed* cutting. [1]
> You look tired, you *need* a rest.
> You *need* to work [1] hard to pass this examination.

Need can have the meaning *want*; in fact in colloquial conversation *want* is often used for *need*, e.g.

> These windows *want* cleaning.
> I never saw such a dirty boy; what he *wants* is a good wash. [2]

The interrogative is made with *do* and the negative with *do not* as with other ordinary verbs, e.g. *Do I need* a haircut ?

> I *don't need* a new suit.
> My hair *didn't need* cutting.

[1] Note the constructions: need + noun or gerund; need + infinitive.
[2] Note the ambiguity of this sentence. The boy may *need* a wash; it's pretty certain he doesn't *want* one; he'd hate it!

235

There is a corresponding noun *need*, e.g.

> I am in *need* of a good car.
> There's no *need* to explain this word.
> There's a real *need* for a book of that sort.
> "A friend in *need* is a friend indeed."

There is an adjective with a negative meaning, *needless*.

> You see, all your worry was quite *needless*.

Note the phrase "needless to say", e.g.

> *Needless to say*, Hob didn't ask for some extra grammar lessons.

II. The second *need* is one of the "specials". It is defective as it has no infinitive, no participles, no past tense. It has the meaning, "to be necessary". Like the other "specials", it makes its interrogative by inversion and its negative by adding *not* (the negative is almost always shortened to *needn't*), and the third person singular does not take "s".

> *Need* I answer that question?
> *Need* he go so soon?
> You *needn't* answer the question.
> He *needn't* go so soon.

A peculiarity of this verb is that it is practically never used in affirmative statements, only in negative ones, or in questions. On the rare occasions when it is used in affirmative statements it is with such words as *hardly*, *scarcely*, which are partly negative in meaning, e.g.

> I *hardly need* say how much I enjoyed my holiday.

Like the other "specials" it can be used in "question phrases", e.g.

> You *needn't* go yet, *need* you?
> I *needn't* tell you the answer, *need* I?

It can, too, be used for short negative answers, e.g.

> Who *needn't* go before eleven o'clock? I *needn't*.
> Is there anyone who *needn't* get up for breakfast? Yes, I *needn't*.

But with affirmative ones you use *must*, e.g.

> *Need* you go before eleven o'clock? Yes, I *must*. (NOT Yes, I *need*.)

It can, like the other "specials", be used in the "neither do I" construction (that is the negative one; it can't be used in the affirmative one "and so do I"), e.g.

> Jan needn't come here tomorrow; *neither need I*.

Like the other specials, it takes the adverbs *never*, *sometimes*, *often*, etc., after it, and not before it as the ordinary verbs do, e.g.

> I needn't *always* get up at seven o'clock.

There is an idiomatic construction illustrating both the verbs *need* that ought to be noted.

FULL VERB: He sent me the money he owed me; so *I didn't need* to write to him for it. (*You gather from this sentence that I didn't write.*)

"SPECIAL": He sent me the money he owed me; so I *needn't have written*. (*You gather from this sentence that I did write.*)

FULL VERB: We had plenty of bread; so I *didn't need* to buy a loaf. (*I didn't buy one.*)

"SPECIAL": We had plenty of bread; so I *needn't have* bought a
loaf. (*I did buy one.*)

FULL VERB: John went to the station with the car to meet Lucille;
so *she didn't need* to walk to the house. (*She didn't walk.*)

"SPECIAL": John went to the station with the car to meet Lucille;
so she *needn't have walked.* (*She did walk.*)

EXERCISES

I. *Make the following sentences negative:*

1. His hair needs cutting.
2. They need a holiday.
3. Henry needed a new bicycle.
4. I need this book for my work.
5. You needed the help that I gave you.

II. *Complete these question phrases:*

1. You needn't write to him, ————?
2. I needn't come tomorrow, ————?
3. He needn't work on Sunday, ————?
4. They needn't waken me so early, ————?
5. We needn't answer all the questions, ————?

III. *Answer the following questions by putting* need *or* must *in the place marked:*

1. Who needn't work for his living? I ————
2. Who needn't catch the early train home? George ————
3. Need you go so soon? Yes, I ————
4. Needn't George go to London tomorrow? No, he ————
5. Need George go to London tomorrow? Yes, he ————
6. Need we read all this lesson? Yes, you ————

IV. *In the following sentences explain how the meaning of* (a) *differs from the meaning of* (b):

1. (a) I didn't need to leave the door unlocked; John had a key.
   (b) I needn't have left the door unlocked; John had a key.
2. (a) She didn't need to tell me the time of the train; I knew it already.
   (b) She needn't have told me the time of the train; I knew it already.
3. (a) He didn't need to take a taxi; it is only five minutes walk to the house.
   (b) He needn't have taken a taxi; it is only five minutes walk to the house.

Composition Exercises

1. "Man is the only animal that can blush—or needs to." What do you think Mark Twain meant by this? Do you agree?

2. Write a short story called "A Friend in Need, is a Friend Indeed."

LESSON 31

Wales and the Welsh

(*Extracts from Jan's Diary*)

. . . What a beautiful country Wales is, and how interesting its people are. We have been here nearly a fortnight now and Mr. Evans has taken us, on foot or in his car, round this countryside which he knows like the back of his hand and loves more than he can ever love any place outside heaven. In fact I shouldn't be surprised, if, when he gets to heaven, he thinks that Wales was practically as good. He and his father and his grandfather, and I don't know how many other generations, have always lived in this little village in North Wales and he knows every man, woman and child for miles around. In fact it almost seems as if everyone in the village is named either Evans or Jones or Hughes, which can lead to some difficulty if you ask for "Mr. Jones's house". Even if you ask, for example, for John Jones, it is almost as bad, for there are probably half a dozen of them. The Welsh people get over this quite well. They don't say just "Mr. Jones", they say "Jones the Milk" (that is the Jones who sells milk) or "Jones the Post" (that's Jones the postman) or "Jones the Bank". So our Mr. Evans being the schoolmaster of the village is "Evans the School".

"But you see," said Mr. Evans, "it's quite natural that you have all these Evanses here; we are all A) related. No one has a deeper love of his home and family than the Welshman, and he doesn't generally go far away from his home. The Englishman has spread his empire to the four corners of the earth; there are probably as many Scotsmen in Canada as there are in Edinburgh; there are more Irishmen in New York than in the whole of Ireland. But the Welshman has never been an empire-builder—in fact, he hasn't been able even to unite his own country. You've probably noticed that until a short time ago [1] there was no capital of Wales as London is the capital of England, Edinburgh of Scotland, Paris of France. Throughout its whole history Wales has always preferred to live in small groupings. The Romans built cities in England and Wales; the English built great castles, and towns grew round them. But the Welsh would have nothing to do with Roman city or English town. The Welsh are countrymen, not townsmen. [2] The family is the centre of Welsh life; this village— like any village here—is just an extended family; and so, as I said, naturally you get a lot of Evanses there.

"You may have heard Welshmen, perhaps in London," he continued " singing *Land of my Fathers*:

> 'Till life is past
> My love shall last
> My longing, my "hiraeth" for Wales.'

[1] In 1956 Cardiff was made the capital.
[2] Mr. Evans is speaking more of North Wales (where he has always lived) than of South Wales. There, the coal and iron industries, and the position of the ports of Cardiff, Swansea and Newport, have led to the growth of big cities and towns and a more "mixed" population.

Land of My Fathers

JAMES JAMES
Arr. by H.A.C.

O land of my fa-thers, dear home-land to me, The mo-ther of po-ets, the land of the free! Thy no-ble de-fend-ers were gal-lant and brave, For free-dom their life's blood they gave. Wales! Wales! Home, sweet home is in Wales. Till life is past, My love shall last, My long-ing, My hi-raeth for Wales!

I can't give you the English for 'hiraeth'; there isn't any English word for it. But it expresses the deep, passionate home-sickness that the Welshman feels for his home. It isn't for 'Wales', in spite of all that our 'Nationalists' may say; it is for some small part of Wales, a tiny village, a valley, a hillside where his family live. For that he would give his life; that is home and 'Wales' to him. The love that he has for that could never be beaten down by Roman or Saxon or Englishman. Until you realise that, I don't think you can understand the character of the Welsh and the spirit of Wales. That was what made us fight against the English; not because we ever wanted to conquer England but because we wanted to keep our homes free, our religion free and to keep the Welsh way of life. That is why the story of King Arthur is a living story with us. When the light of Christianity that the Romans had brought to England was put out by the heathen Saxons who invaded the country, it was Arthur who battled against them, and it was the Welsh who kept Christianity alive in these islands. Have you noticed—I am sure you must have done— the number of Welsh place names that begin with 'Llan'—Llanberis, Llandudno, Llangollen, Llanfair, there are hundreds of them in Wales ? Well, in those dark days of the early Saxon occupation of England, Christianity still lived on among the Welsh, and specially chosen men, the first Celtic saints, went from place to place teaching the Christian faith, preaching, organising little groups of believers, and starting centres of worship. These centres were called *llans* (the word is generally translated *church*), and the *llans* often took the name of the saint who started them or some other holy name; for example, Llandudno was the *llan* started by St. Tudno, Llandewi was the *llan* of St. Ddewi (David), Llanfair was the *llan* of Fair (Mary).

"Everyone knows the story of how Christianity was brought to England by St. Augustine. (It's quite a good story, as *English* stories go, though not to be compared with the Welsh ones.) But not so many people realise that there was a cathedral in Wales, the Cathedral of St. David, that was built in A.D. 550, forty-seven years before St. Augustine came to Canterbury. And the Welsh are still, as they always were, a deeply religious people."

I hardly needed to be told that. Every village seems to have two or three "Chapels"—usually extremely ugly buildings—and on Sunday a great silence falls over the village. No shops are open, no work is done, no games are played. The men that I had seen during the week in rough working clothes come out now dressed in formal black with white collars to go to the chapel. The chapels are crowded and the whole congregation is a choir, for these Welsh people can certainly sing. The sermon, listened to by a deeply interested and highly critical congregation, lasts an hour.

"I know you think our chapels are ugly," said Mr. Evans, voicing my unspoken thoughts, "but for us Welsh a church is above all else a place for worship, not an exercise in beautiful architecture. Besides, the Welsh have always been a poor people and could never afford magnificent churches. But it is in those chapels that our religion, our Welsh language and all the things that make us proud to be Welshmen have been kept alive."

Oh yes, they are a great people.

EXERCISES

I. *Use the following words and phrases in sentences:*

1. like the back of his hand
2. Heaven
3. generations
4. natural
5. empire
6. unite
7. throughout its history
8. have nothing to do with
9. passionate
10. occupation
11. organise
12. holy
13. not to be compared with
14. realise
15. cathedral
16. religious
17. congregation
18. ugly
19. formal
20. critical

II. *Answer these questions:*

1. There are many people with the same name in a Welsh village. How do the Welsh get over this difficulty?
2. Why haven't many Welshmen gone abroad?
3. What is the English for (a) "llan", (b) "hiraeth"?
4. Why are Welsh chapels often ugly?
5. Why was Mr. Evans not worried by the ugliness of some of the chapels?
6. How long does the sermon usually last?
7. How does Mr. Evans earn his living? What is he called by his neighbours?

III. *Choose the correct word from these in brackets:*

1. We have (be, been, are) here nearly a (fortnight, two weeks).
2. Nearly (all, everyone, every) in the village seems to be (either, neither, both) Evans or Jones or Hughes.
3. There are probably as (much, more, many) Scotsmen in Canada (than, as, also) there are in Edinburgh.
4. All Welshmen have a (good, deep, high) love for (his, their) home.
5. The (town, house, family) is the centre of village (live, life).
6. When the Saxons (fought, invade, invaded) the land, it was the Welsh (who, by whom, whose) kept Christianity alive.
7. Frieda and Jan (can't, hadn't, didn't) know the story (of, to, on) St. Augustine.
8. The Welsh (never, often, still) are a deeply religious people.
9. Jan would like to (go, visit, journey) Wales (again, ever).
10. I think he (would, will) like Frieda to go (from, with, of) him also.

IV. *Using the phrases given and adding words of your own, make the following into complete sentences:*

1. Jan found . . . beautiful country . . . interesting people.
2. many trips . . . on foot . . . the countryside.
3. don't often leave . . . because . . . their homes . . . everything else.
4. what made us fight . . . to conquer . . . homes free.
5. quite . . . good story . . . as English stories . . . not to be compared.
6. how much . . . one pound . . . tomatoes . . . window?
7. large crowds . . . at the station . . . the Queen.
8. those sandwiches . . . restaurant . . . expensive.
9. Hob . . . oughtn't . . . chocolates.
10. run . . . post office . . . telegram.

V. *Give short questions to which the following are answers:*

1. Yes, you may.
2. At six o'clock.
3. I left it on the table.
4. No, I can't.
5. I hope to go tomorrow.
6. Only one of your sentences is right.
7. Yes, he must.
8. It's raining hard.
9. He's a schoolmaster.
10. No sugar, thank you.
11. It costs 22½ pence.
12. No, they don't.
13. Very well, thank you.
14. Very much, thank you.
15. I feel much better today.
16. It's made of nylon.
17. We hope to go to Italy.
18. No, we haven't.
19. But, I have tidied my room.
20. And so have I.

Composition Exercises

1. Describe how your religion first came to your country.

2. Why are the Welsh not great empire-builders?

3. Read again the passage on pages 241 and 243 marked (A) . . . (B) and then write a précis of it in about 200 words.

LESSON 32

The "Special" Verbs (ix): Dare, Used (to)

MR. PRIESTLEY: There are three specials that we haven't already studied and I want to finish two of them off today.[1] The first of them is *dare*. As you can see from these examples, it can form its interrogative and negative, its "question phrases" and "short answers"[2] like the other specials.

Dare you climb that tree?
Dare[3] he go and speak to her?
How *dare* you say such a thing?
You *daren't* climb that tree, *dare you*? Yes, I *dare*.
He *daren't* go and speak to her.
I have never *dared* to do that.

But *dare* can also form its negative like the usual verbs, i.e. with *do (did) not*.

She *didn't dare* to say a word.
He *doesn't dare* to answer my letter.
We *didn't dare* to ask if we could have a holiday.

Note that in these cases the *to* of the infinitive of the verb that follows *dare* is not omitted.

---

[1] The remaining one, *must*, is dealt with fully in Book IV.

[2] The constructions " and so — " and " neither — " are not often used with *dare* and *need* (but see p. 237, ll. 13–15). They are never used with *used to*. The adverbs *always, sometimes, never*, etc., come *after* these verbs, not before them.

[3] Note there is no "s" in the 3rd person singular.

In all the examples just given, the meaning of *dare you?* = "have you courage enough?", "are you brave enough?" There is another slightly different meaning, a meaning "to challenge", e.g.

> I *dared him* to ask for a holiday tomorrow.
> He *dared me* to walk down Piccadilly in my pyjamas.
> *Do you dare me* to swim to that rock and back again?

Here, as you see, *dare* has a personal object (*him*, *me*, etc.) and is conjugated with *do* and is followed by an infinitive with *to*.

Just one other expression should be noticed: *I daresay*, which simply means *perhaps*, *it is probable*.

> He is not here yet, but I *daresay* he will come later.
> They haven't widened this road yet, but I *daresay* they will some day.
> Do you think Alice will come and see us today? Oh, I *daresay*.

The expression is not used with any pronoun except *I*.

Used (to)[1]

Used [ju:st] only just manages to get into the group of specials. Undoubtedly it is peculiar; for example, there is no other form of it except *used*, and the usual grammar books will tell you that the interrogative is *used you?* and the negative *usen't*. But we are all rather doubtful about it. You will hear:

> You *used to* live in London, *usen't you?*
> He *usen't* to smoke as much as he does now.

---

[1] You have already met this verb in *Essential English*, Book I, p. 182.

I

There *used to* be an old apple tree in the garden. Oh, *used there?*

Used you to climb the old apple tree in the garden?

You usen't to make that mistake.

But the tendency is more and more in spoken English to say:

You *used to* live in London, *didn't* you?[1]

He *didn't use* to smoke as much as he does now.

There *used to* be an old apple tree in the garden. Oh, *did there?*

Did you use to climb the old apple tree in the garden?

You *didn't use* to make that mistake.

We still feel uneasy about using *do* and *did*, and in negative sentences we often try to avoid the difficulty by using *never*:

You *never used* to make that mistake.

He *never used* to smoke as much, etc.

In all those sentences *used* expressed something that was usual or habitual in the past, e.g.

I *used* to work in London but I don't work there now, I work in Manchester.

You will note that the present tense of:

"I *used to work* (in London)" is NOT

"Now I *use to work* (in Manchester)" but the Simple Present Tense, "Now I *work* (in Manchester)."

Don't confuse *used* with this meaning and *used to* ['juːz tə] meaning "accustomed to", e.g.

Adam the gardener works better than I do in the garden. He's *used to* doing hard work. I'm not *used to* hard work, but I'll get *used to* it in time.

[1] With question phrases the form with *do* (*did*) is practically always used.

Your cat, Sally, won't sit on my knee as she does on yours. Well, she's *used to* me, she's not *used to* you.

You will see from the above examples how we *use* the phrase *used to* (= accustomed to). It is always followed by an object ("hard work", "it", "me", "you") or a gerund, e.g. "working", "doing", etc.

Nor must you confuse *used to* with the verb: *use* [ju:z], or the past participle of this verb *used* [ju:zd], e.g.

> I *use* the same shaving brush now that I have *used* for ten years.
> I think you have *used* your time well while you have been in England.

And that, I think, is the end for the time being of the lessons on "The Specials".

EXERCISES

I. *Answer the following questions in the negative:*

1. Dare you speak to her?
2. Dare the children drive the car alone?
3. Will he dare to come?
4. Did he dare to swim across the river?
5. Usen't you to go to school with John?
6. Didn't you use to go to school with John?
7. Usen't he to work in Liverpool?
8. Didn't he use to work in Liverpool?
9. Are you used to getting up early?
10. Used you to get up early when you were at home?
11. Is Lucille used to driving that car?
12. Usen't she to have a smaller car than that?

II. *Explain the difference in meaning between:*

      (*a*) He dared to swim across the river.

and (*b*) He dared me to swim across the river.

      (*a*) She dared to ask the teacher for a holiday.

and (*b*) She dared me to ask the teacher for a holiday.

III. *Add "question phrases" to each of the following:*

1. You daren't do that, ————?
2. He didn't dare to do that, ————?
3. He won't dare to do that, ————?
4. He dared you to do that, ————?
5. You used to live there, ————?
6. He usen't to work in London, ————?
7. He never used to spend so much money before he knew Lucille, ————?
8. You used to like dancing, ————?
9. He daren't say what he thinks, ————?
10. He didn't dare to say what he thought, ————?

LESSON 33

The Eisteddfod

(*Extracts from Jan's diary*)

. . . I think the last two days have been two of the most interesting days I have ever spent. I have seen a Welsh Eisteddfod, a national gathering of an enormous crowd of people devoted to music and poetry. The Welsh are a nation of singers. Wherever you get a crowd of Welshmen, whether they're down the mine, in the factory or waiting on the platform for a train, they just can't help bursting into song. "Anyone," said Mr. Evans, "who has heard a crowd of 50,000 Welshmen before a Rugby match at Cardiff singing 'Land of my Fathers', will never forget it." You could hardly find a town in Wales, however small, that hasn't a choir. Its conductor isn't a trained musician; he may be only a miner, an agricultural labourer or "Jones the milk"; but the university lecturer or the doctor's daughter will be happy to work under his leadership. The choir will gather in the little chapel almost every night for practice—for they are preparing for the Eisteddfod, and the pieces set for competition (this year they are two difficult works by Bach and Brahms) need a lot of practice to bring them to perfection. I should think the Welsh are the only people in the world whose only national festival is devoted to music and poetry. For that is what an Eisteddfod is. Their National Eisteddfod[1] is held every year in the first week in August, one year in the North of Wales, the next year in the South, and competitors come from all parts of Wales to compete in it. For twelve months thousands of Welsh people have been practising music; the shepherd on the hills, the teacher in the grammar school have been working at the poem that they hope will win the prize. A housewife may be a harpist, a parson a poet. During the week of the competition about a hundred thousand people will travel to the Eisteddfod to hear the competitors and listen to the judges' decisions.

The Eisteddfod is one of the oldest of all Welsh customs; the first one of which we have any record was held in the 6th century, and as early as A.D. 940 the prize for the winning "bard" (poet) was a chair or throne. And that is still the prize today. In medieval times every chieftain used to keep a bard, and there were other bards who wandered about the country singing songs and making poems. There must have been quite a lot of poor singing and bad poetry then, for Queen Elizabeth I ordered an Eisteddfod to be held every year with the object of raising the standard of music and getting rid of the lazy, worthless bards.

By a stroke of great good fortune for Frieda and me, the Eisteddfod was due to take place this year at Caernarvon at the very time that we were in North Wales. Mr. Evans has a brother who lives in Caernarvon and he invited us to stay at his house the night before the meeting opened, "For," said Mr. Evans, "we must be up early tomorrow morning to see the

[1] There are lots of local ones held in various towns throughout the year.

Gorsedd." "What's a Gorsedd?" I asked. "You'll see, tomorrow," he replied.

So, early next morning we all went to a large grassy field or park just outside Caernarvon. The streets were busy with people and in the field there was a large crowd gathered round a circle of big stones, with an "altar stone" in the middle, like Stonehenge.

STONEHENGE

Soon I could see a procession coming slowly towards the stone circle. And very colourful it was. First there were four men carrying on their shoulders a kind of platform on which was an enormous golden horn. ("That's the 'Hirlas Horn', the Horn of Plenty", said Mr. Evans. "It's kept all the year in the museum at Cardiff.") Behind them walked men in white robes. ("The Druids," said Mr. Evans. "Druidism was a culture and a religion that existed in Wales in the very earliest times. Caesar and Tacitus wrote about the Druids against whom the Romans fought in Anglesey. They were white-robed priests and law-givers who held their meetings in the woods where they offered up human sacrifices. One of their ceremonies was the cutting of the mistletoe that grew on the oak-trees in Anglesey—a custom that we still remember at Christmas-time. At one time it was believed that the Druids had built the great stone circles that are still seen at Stonehenge and in other parts of Britain, but those stone circles are much older than that.")

By this time the " Druids " had come to the stone circle and now stood in a double row before the altar stone. And then, between the lines of Druids came a man dressed in green and carrying a long two-handed sword. Behind him came a tall, bearded man in white, and wearing a great breastplate. "The Chief Druid," whispered Mr. Evans. A friendly Welshman next to me pointed to one of the "bards". "That's Cadwallo," he said "a great poet." I looked at the man he had pointed to and said to Mr. Evans, "But that's the Rev. J. A. Hughes, our parson at Capel Curig, isn't it ?" "Yes," he said, "but all our great poets are known by their 'bardic' names."

Then the ceremony of the Gorsedd began. The sword-bearer drew the great sword from its sheath. One by one the Druids came forward and put their hands on it. Then the Chief Druid called out in a loud voice something in Welsh. "He says, 'Is it peace ?'" whispered Mr. Evans. The Chief Druid shouted this three times, and each time the crowd called back, "It is peace." A woman dressed in red and carrying the golden horn came forward to the Chief Druid. He touched it, and she slowly walked back to her place. Then the Chief Druid stepped on to the altar stone and made a long speech in Welsh. I didn't understand a word of it but the audience loved it. Other bards spoke and the crowd enjoyed every minute of it. Then there were prayers in Welsh and, at the end of this, new bards, men and women dressed in blue robes, were brought before the Chief Druid. These were people who had done some particularly good work in poetry or music. The Chief Druid shook hands with them and gave each of them a bardic name by which he would be called at all future Gorsedds. Then the procession formed again; the great sword was held high above the heads of the people; bards and Druids moved off slowly; the crowds began to fade away; the Eisteddfod was opened.

*　　　*　　　*　　　*

In the afternoon we went to the Eisteddfod. An enormous tent had been put up. "It holds 10,000 people," said Mr. Evans, "that's as many as the Albert Hall in London holds." There were thousands of people there, going into the Eisteddfod tent or sitting on the grass outside. We took our places inside. The three best competitors in each event had been chosen in "preliminary" trials, and now soloists and choirs came in turn to sing, to play the harp, to speak their poems, while the judges listened and, at the end of the event, announced the winner and gave reasons for their choice. Though I enjoyed the music I couldn't understand anything else, for at the Eisteddfod everything is done in Welsh. One of the most interesting competitions (at least for those who understand Welsh) is "pennillion" singing. In this the competitors are accompanied on the harp and have to make up their song as they go along.

But the great event comes at the end. This is the

THE OPENING OF THE EISTEDDFOD

choosing of the " crowned bard ", the greatest honour the Eisteddfod can give. For a whole year bards have been working at a poem on a subject that has been set by the judges. These poems have been sent to the judges before the Eisteddfod starts and have been carefully studied by the Council of the Druids. I looked round the scene. The tent was now crowded, every seat was taken and people were standing in the passageways. There was a tremendous feeling of excitement and expectation. The trumpets sounded, and in procession came all the bards that we had seen at the Gorsedd. The Chief Druid took his seat in the centre. Again the trumpets sounded and in a silence that you could almost feel the Chief Druid said, "The Crown has been won by . . . (*there was a pause*) CADWALLO."

There was a great burst of cheering. The audience were on their feet. Mr. Evans was jumping about with excitement and joy; the crown had been won by Mr. Hughes, the parson of his village. I could see Mr. Hughes at the back of the tent. Two bards from the platform went towards him and, one at each side of him, brought him to the platform. He was told to sit on a finely-carved chair of Druid's oak that is to be his prize. They put a robe of purple on him with white fur at the edges. The great sword was held over him, and the Chief Druid came forward and put a crown on his head. The Chief Bard read the poem that Cadwallo had written and, though of course I couldn't understand it, the crowd clearly agreed completely with the Druids' decision.

So the Eisteddfod ended.

And our holiday in Wales has ended, too; tomorrow we leave for London and work again.

*   *   *

Frieda has bought a little silver Welsh harp to wear as a brooch; you'll see it when she gets back.

EXERCISES

I. *Use the following words and phrases in sentences:*

1. devoted to	12. was due to	21. tent
2. mine (noun)	13. procession	22. trial
3. Rugby match	14. shoulders	23. accompany
4. agricultural	15. horn	24. tremendous
5. labourer	16. human	25. trumpet
6. under his	sacrifices	26. purple
leadership	17. row (noun)	27. fur
7. competition	18. every minute	28. at the edges
8. perfection	of it	29. at each side of
9. shepherd	19. robe	him
10. parson	20. fade away	30. brooch
11. worthless		

II. *Say in one or two sentences what the following do:*

1. a miner; 2. a housewife; 3. an agricultural labourer; 4. a parson; 5. a doctor; 6. a schoolmaster; 7. a postman; 8. a milkman; 9. a shepherd; 10. a porter.

III. *Answer these questions:*

1. Are the conductors of Welsh choirs usually trained musicians?
2. What is an Eisteddfod?
3. What sort of people take part in an Eisteddfod?

4. Where do they come from?
5. When was the first Eisteddfod held?
6. Where and when does the Eisteddfod take place nowadays?
7. Do you think the Druids built Stonehenge?
8. Where is the Hirlas horn usually kept?
9. Why did Queen Elizabeth I order an Eisteddfod to be held?
10. Why didn't Jan understand anything at the Eisteddfod?
11. Who was Cadwallo?
12. What Christmas custom began with the Druids?
13. What do you think is the Welsh national musical instrument? (Frieda might help you.)
14. Why are the poems sent to the judges before the Eisteddfod begins?
15. What happens to the winner of the crown?

IV. *Choose the correct word from those in brackets:*

1. The Welsh are a nation of (sailors, singers, servants).
2. A choir (sees, accompanies, gathers) in the chapel for (poetry, a Rugby match, practice).
3. Anyone who has (hearing, hear, heard) a crowd of 50,000 singing at Cardiff will never (forgotten, forget, remember) it.
4. The Welsh are the (only, whole, all) people in the world (who, whom, whose) only national festival is devoted (by, from, to) music and poetry.
5. One year it is (in, near, to) the North of Wales, the (first, second, next) year in the South.
6. A housewife (should, may, will) be a harpist.
7. I don't (forget, understand, understood) a word of Welsh, but the (bards, audiences, Chief Druid) love it all.
8. The competitors have to (make, made, take) up their song as they (went, go, sing) along.
9. Jan can (see, saw, seeing) a (row, procession) coming towards him.
10. Frieda is (bought, brought, buying) a small brooch for (her, herself, she).

V. *Rewrite the sentences of No.* IV *in the past tense.*

VI. *The following is half a conversation between Jan and Frieda in the evening of the day at the Eisteddfod. Can you put in what Jan might have said to Frieda?*

FRIEDA: That was a lovely day, wasn't it?

JAN: ———————

FRIEDA: Yes, if we'd been a week later we shouldn't have seen it at all.

JAN: ———————

FRIEDA: I thought it was when Cadwallo won, and everybody cheered. What did you think was the best moment?

JAN: ———————

FRIEDA: Yes, I thought that was good too. I liked the part when the procession came.

JAN: ———————

FRIEDA: And it was also most impressive.

JAN: ———————

FRIEDA: I'm glad I didn't live in those days when they had human sacrifices. I say, Jan, what's the time?

JAN: ———————

FRIEDA: Oh, good, let's go for a walk along the valley before supper.

JAN: ———————

Composition Exercises

1. Describe what happens at the Gorsedd.

2. Describe any festival of music that is held in your country.

3. Write a letter that Frieda might have written to Mr. Priestley describing the crowning of the bard.

4. Queen Elizabeth I wanted to get rid of "worthless poets". Do you think poets today are useful and give pleasure, or do you think we don't need them? Give reasons for your answer.

LESSON 34

Punctuation

OLAF: If I write: "The castle which was built in the 13th century is one of the finest in Britain", ought I to put a comma after *castle* and after *century*?

MR. PRIESTLEY: Yes.

HOB: I never bother about commas. I don't see that they matter at all.

MR. PRIESTLEY: Don't you, Hob? Let me tell you a little story.

One day, as a teacher walked into his classroom, he heard Tommy Andrews whisper to the boy next to him: "Here's the teacher. I'll bet the silly donkey is going to talk about putting in commas." The teacher didn't say anything but he began to talk about putting in commas, and explained how important they could be. To show what he meant, he wrote on the blackboard the sentence:

"Tommy Andrews says the teacher is a silly donkey."

The class laughed and Tommy Andrews looked very red. "Now," said the teacher, "I will show you how important commas are." He put two commas into the sentence, and it now read:

"Tommy Andrews, says the teacher, is a silly donkey."

PEDRO: I like the story about the barber who put a notice outside his shop:

> What do you think I
> shave you for nothing
> and give you a drink

Of course he soon had his shop full of men all expecting to be shaved for nothing and then given a glass of beer. But the barber explained that that wasn't what he meant. A little punctuation made all the difference, for the notice then read:

> What! Do you think I
> shave you for nothing,
> and give you a drink?

MR. PRIESTLEY: Punctuation can often say quite a lot. There is a story of the great French novelist, Victor Hugo. When his first book was published, he wondered if it had been a success, so he sent a postcard to his publisher with just a question mark on it (?). The publisher's reply was equally short. It was an exclamation mark (!).

LUCILLE: My favourite punctuation story is about the wife of a man who had just joined the Navy during the war, and, on Sunday, his wife handed a little note to the parson which read:

> "Peter Smith having gone to sea his wife would like
> your prayers for his safety."

She had forgotten to put in the comma after the word *sea*, and the parson, without thinking, read:

> "Peter Smith having gone to see his wife would like your prayers for his safety."

MR. PRIESTLEY: Well, Hob, do you still think that commas don't matter?

JAN: Could you please give us a lesson on the rules of punctuation? There are a lot of things about punctuation that I am not sure about.

MR. PRIESTLEY: I think the following points might be useful:

Many of the most commonly used punctuation marks are illustrated in the examples I have just given you; these are **Quotation marks** or inverted commas (" "), used to show direct speech; the **Exclamation mark** (!), used after an interjection or expression of strong feeling; the **Question mark** (?), used after a direct question, but not after an indirect one; the **Comma** (,) and the **Full stop** (.).

The full stop, the semi-colon (;) and the comma are generally used to show the pause that you would make in speaking the words. The full stop marks the longest pause; the comma, the shortest pause; the semi-colon marks a longer pause than the comma.

The **Full stop** is used:

(1) at the end of all sentences, except questions and exclamations, e.g.

> He needs your help. (*Statement*)
> Help him. (*Command*)

Will you help him? (*Question*)
He cried, "Help! Help!" (*Exclamation*)

(2) After abbreviations such as M.A. (= Master of Arts), H.M.S. *Valiant* (= Her Majesty's Ship *Valiant*), U.S.A. (= United States of America), e.g. (=*exempli gratia* (Latin) = for example), etc.

The **Colon** is used:

(1) to separate sentences of which the second explains more fully the meaning of the first. It often means the same as "that is to say", e.g.

> Richard's work is unsatisfactory: his answers are thoughtless, his spelling is careless and his writing is bad.

(2) to introduce a number of items in a list, e.g.

> Some commonly used punctuation marks are:
> full stop, colon, semi-colon and comma.

The **Semi-colon** is useful when we need a longer pause than is indicated by a comma, but when we don't want to break the line of thought, as would happen if we used a full stop. It is used:

(1) to separate sentences, especially when a conjunction is not used, e.g.

> "Your appearance pleased my friend; then it delighted me; I have watched your behaviour in strange circumstances; I have studied how you played and how you bore your losses; lastly, I have asked you to do a most dangerous thing, and you received it like an invitation to dinner."
>
> R. L. STEVENSON.

Note how, in this example, shorter pauses are shown by the commas.

(2) with words like *so, therefore, however, nevertheless, besides, then, otherwise*. These words join sentences but are stronger than mere conjunctions like *and* or *but*, and so need a stronger punctuation mark. Here are some examples:

> Do the work well; then I will pay you.
> You must take more exercise; otherwise you will get too fat.
> Richard didn't work hard; so he didn't pass his examination.

The **Comma** is the most frequently used punctuation mark and has many uses. Your common sense and the desire to make your meaning clear will often tell you where you want to make a pause, but the following "rules", though they don't cover all the uses, may be helpful.

A comma is generally used:

(1) to record a list of objects, etc., e.g.

> At the party we had cakes, jellies, ices, biscuits, chocolate and lemonade.[1]

(2) to mark off direct speech:

> "Tell me," he said, "how you know all that."
> The man replied, "I heard it on the radio."

(3) to mark off sentences or clauses where a pause is needed in reading. This is almost always the case if the clause is an adverb one, e.g.

> Although it was foggy, we played the match.
> I have explained this work to Richard, but he still doesn't understand it.
> If you will help me, I will help you.
> John, who is in our class, has won a scholarship.

[1] Notice that the comma is not usually put before *and* and the last item.

(4) to mark off words used in addressing a person, e.g.

> George, tell Richard the answer to the question.
> I hope, sir, my answer is right.

(5) to mark off words or phrases like *however*, *therefore*, *of course*, *for instance*, etc.

> You know, of course, what a gerund is; I needn't, therefore, explain it now.

(6) in descriptive titles such as:

> Elizabeth II, Queen of Great Britain, was born in 1926.
> I saw Mr. Smith, your teacher, this morning.

(7) to mark off phrases containing a participle when a pause is required in reading:

> George, seeing that his brother was hurt, ran to help him.
> Remembering how fond you are of fruit, I've brought you some apples from our garden.

EXERCISE

Rewrite the following stories, and put in the punctuation:

(i)

The following was written on the gravestone of an army mule here lies maggie the mule who in her time kicked a general two colonels four majors ten captains twenty-four lieutenants forty sergeants two hundred and twenty privates and a bomb.

(ii)

i cant understand it said mr williams oh what cant you understand said his friend well said mr williams just look at this suit im wearing the wool was grown in australia the cloth was woven in yorkshire the buttons were made in india the suit was made in london and i bought it in cairo whats so remarkable about that asked his friend isnt it wonderful said williams taking no notice of the interruption that so many people can make a living out of something i havent paid for

(iii)

a very agitated woman rang up her doctor and a servant answered the phone can i speak to dr russell she said its urgent im sorry madam the doctor is out will you leave a message oh dear oh dear my ten year old little boy has swallowed a fountain pen when will the doctor be in im afraid madam he wont be in for two hours perhaps three hours three hours cried the woman what shall i do in the meantime im afraid madam youll have to use a pencil

(iv)

the mayfair club for noblemen and gentlemen was famous one day a member who had lost his umbrella there went to the secretary and asked him to put up a notice which read will the nobleman who took an umbrella that did not belong to him please return it at once but why nobleman asked the surprised secretary well was the answer this is a club for noblemen and gentlemen and the person who took my umbrella was certainly no gentleman

LESSON 35

The Body

HOB, PEDRO, LUCILLE, OLAF, FRIEDA, JAN

HOB: In most of the books that I have seen for learning English there's a lesson on "Parts of the Body" to give you all the vocabulary. Here's one, by Professor Dryasdust, with a picture. That will show you what I mean. Mr. Priestley has never given us a lesson like that.

LUCILLE: And a jolly good thing, too; I can't think of anything more boring.

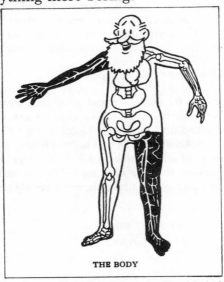

THE BODY

This is the picture that Hob brought to the class. It is from Professor Dryasdust's book *English for Ruritanians* and is printed here by kind permission of the Professor's publishers, Messrs. Apfelstrudl & Co. Strelsau.

OLAF: Besides we know all those words: *head, arm, leg, nose*. It would be a waste of time.

HOB: All the same I'm going to ask Mr. Priestley for a lesson like that.

*   *   *   *

(A little later. Hob has asked for a lesson on "The Body". Mr. Priestley has listened to Hob's request and the objections of the other students.)

MR. PRIESTLEY: I think there is a way of letting Hob have the lesson he wants (after all, it's not often that he *wants* a lesson) and yet of not boring you all. There are a good many idioms, which may be new to you, belonging to "parts of the body", so what I suggest is this: Hob can use his picture and give us the vocabulary, then any of you can supply an idiom, using the word Hob has given us. If none of you can give one, I'll try to do so. Is that all right?

PEDRO: I think that sounds a most interesting and useful idea.

MR. PRIESTLEY: Very good. Well, Hob, you can begin.

HOB: I have a **head**.

PEDRO: "Tom was *head over heels* in love with Helen."[1]

FRIEDA: Hob can do good work, when *he takes it into his head* to try.

JAN: When you are in danger, the important thing is never to *lose your head*.

MR. PRIESTLEY: You are doing so well at this that I am afraid success may *turn your heads*. Go on, Hob.

[1] *Essential English*, Book I, page 177.

HOB: I have a **neck**.

OLAF: I don't know who is going to win this competition in idioms; I think we are running *neck and neck*.

FRIEDA: I don't know many idioms, but I'll have a try. It's *neck or nothing*.

HOB: If you don't do better than that you'll *get it in the neck*[1] from Mr. Priestley.

MR. PRIESTLEY: Continue, Hob.

HOB: I have two **eyes**.

LUCILLE: I can see that with *half an eye*.

OLAF: Will you accept a proverb, sir, instead of an idiom? If you will, I'll give you: " In the country of the blind, the *one-eyed* man is King."

MR. PRIESTLEY: Well, we may not *see eye to eye* about that, Olaf, but we'll let it pass.

JAN: I'm *up to the eyes* in work, but I want to find time to play football on Saturday.

FRIEDA: And when you see what a good footballer Jan is, it will *make you open your eyes*.

HOB: That's *all my eye!*[2] Did I ever tell you the story of the man who was *cross-eyed*—and very bad-tempered?

He was hurrying along a crowded street one day and knocked into a man who was coming the opposite way.

"Why don't you look where you are going?" the cross-eyed man burst out angrily.

"And why don't you go where you are looking?" answered the other.

MR. PRIESTLEY: All right, Hob, but get on with the job.

---

[1] This is slang.   [2] Hob's idiom is slang.

HOB: I have a **nose**.

LUCILLE: And you like to *poke your nose into other people's business*.

HOB: You may *turn up your nose at me*, Lucille, but I'm bringing my cousin Belinda to our next party. Talk about a beauty! You'll need to *keep an eye on* your boy-friends or Belinda will *put your nose out of joint*.

MR. PRIESTLEY: Come on, Hob. *Keep your nose to the grindstone* and give us the next word.

HOB: I have (what Lucille hasn't) a **heart**. But when you ask me about my homework, *my heart goes into my mouth*—and then *goes into my boots*.

LUCILLE: I'm sorry, Hob. I don't want you to *take* too much *to heart* what I said. I was only joking.

HOB: Of course, Lucille, so was I. I know there isn't a *better-hearted* person than you anywhere—and I say that *with my hand on my heart*.

MR. PRIESTLEY: Well, now that Lucille and Hob have had that little *heart to heart* talk, may we have another word, Hob?

HOB: There's my **shoulder**. That'll beat you.

(*They are all silent*)

MR. PRIESTLEY: That's a difficult one. I'd better take the burden of that *on my shoulders* (though I'm not so *broad-shouldered* as Olaf). But if we all *put our shoulder to the wheel*, we'll get over the difficulty.

HOB: I have a **tongue**—and I expect you often wish I'd *hold* it.

LUCILLE: Well, you *have a sharp tongue* at times, but I

prefer people who are *sharp-tongued* to those who
are too *smooth-tongued*.

JAN: I know another idiom, it's *on the tip of my tongue*
but I can't quite say it.

MR. PRIESTLEY: There's a look on Jan's face that
makes me think he's *speaking with his tongue in
his cheek*. Give us another word, Hob.

HOB: I was going to say **tooth** (teeth) but I'd like to
tell you a story first about a man who had *false
teeth*. He went away for a holiday, and his wife,
knowing how easily they can be lost if you are
bathing in a rough sea, wrote to him, saying,
"Take care not to wear your new teeth when
you are bathing in the sea." He wrote back,
"Why didn't you telegraph?"

MR. PRIESTLEY: Hob certainly works *tooth and nail* to
get his stories told, doesn't he?

HOB: Well, I nearly missed telling you that one; I just
got it in *by the skin of my teeth*. Now what about
my **ears**? I'm listening for your answers *with all
my ears*—and I'm not deaf.

JAN: "There are none so deaf as those who won't
hear." (*Proverb*.)

OLAF: I remember that you said that anything you
told your landlady *went in at one ear and out at the
other*.[1]

MR. PRIESTLEY: Pass on, Hob.

HOB: There are my **fingers** and my **thumbs**, eight
fingers and two thumbs;—though when I
dropped one of his best wine-glasses, Uncle
Albert said that my *fingers were all thumbs*.

[1] Book II, page 135.

LUCILLE: And then, of course, you *like to have a finger in every pie*.

PEDRO: I'm struck by the way Hob always has a story at his *finger-tips*.

MR. PRIESTLEY: All right, Hob, carry on.

HOB: Let's come to my **bones**. There's **flesh** on them and in my veins there is **blood.**

LUCILLE: And some of Hob's stories are about as much as *flesh and blood* can stand.

HOB: I sometimes think that the only person who really appreciates my jokes is Uncle Albert, but, of course, he's my own *flesh and blood*.

MR. PRIESTLEY: And, as they say, *blood is thicker than water*. But find us another word, Hob.

HOB: There's my **hair**. And that's where I have the advantage over Uncle Albert; he's *losing his hair* and going bald.

LUCILLE: I hope, in spite of what I've said, that you'll *keep your hair on*[1] with me, Hob.

HOB: I hope so! If I didn't, it couldn't *stand on end* as it generally does when I'm in your car and you are driving at sixty miles an hour.

LUCILLE: You should be like Pedro. I can do eighty miles an hour when he's in the car, and he doesn't *turn a hair*.

MR. PRIESTLEY: In spite of the many *hair-breadth escapes* he must have had! Let's have one more word, Hob, and that, I'm afraid will be the last.

HOB: Then let's take my **foot**.

MR. PRIESTLEY: Very well, now *put your best foot forward* and see what you can do with this word.

[1] This is slang.

OLAF: I'd like to say something but I'm afraid I'll *put my foot in it*.

HOB: Uncle Albert says that every time I open my mouth I *put my foot in it*.

JAN: As time is short, we mustn't *let the grass grow under our feet*.

FRIEDA: After I had 'flu that holiday in Devon really *set me on my feet*.

HOB: That's what Uncle Albert's "fiver" did for me![1] After I got that, I was able to *stand on my own feet* again.

MR. PRIESTLEY: Well, we must stop there.

HOB: But there are lots of other words in Professor Dryasdust's vocabulary: *skin*, *nails*, *waist*, *beard*, *lips*, *throat*, *wrist*, *knee*, *toe*, *heel*—not to mention my *brains*.

MR. PRIESTLEY: Sorry, Hob, but we must leave it now.

HOB: But ——

MR. PRIESTLEY: No. This is where I *put my foot down* and say the lesson is over. You can stay and study your picture and vocabulary but we are going (on *tip-toe* so that we shan't disturb your studies) to have our lunch.[2]

---

[1] Hob is thinking of his story in Book II, p. 165.
[2] There are more "body idioms" in Book IV.

EXERCISES

I. *Use the following words and phrases in sentences:*

1. boring
2. a waste of time
3. request
4. objections
5. heel
6. accept
7. poke
8. burden
9. pie
10. veins
11. bald
12. disturb
13. appreciate
14. at sixty miles an hour
15. telegraph

II. *Complete these sentences by using an idiom about the word in brackets:*

1. Grandma Wiggins is very (tongue) as Mr. Wiggins knows only too well.
2. The boys were running (neck), but Andrew just won. I hope that the win won't (head).
3. John said he was (eyes) in work.
4. The teacher told the boy that he must (foot) and get on with his work, but I'm afraid (ear).
5. We caught the train (teeth). When we reach Bath we must get out quickly to catch our bus. We must not (feet).
6. This concerns me. I wish you wouldn't (nose).
7. When driving, Lucille never (head), though her passengers sometimes feel (heart, mouth).
8. I had a (heart) talk with the manager and I'm sure he wasn't (tongue, cheek).
9. The Welsh fought (tooth) for their freedom.
10. Though I don't always see (eye) with my cousin, I am going into business with him because (blood).

III. *Put the idioms or proverbs in these sentences into your own words, showing that you understand their meaning:*

1. He likes to have *a finger in every pie.*
2. When Mr. Priestley made the hen-house it seemed as though *his fingers were all thumbs.*

3. "There are none so deaf as those who won't hear." (*Proverb.*)

4. I could see *with half an eye* that all was not well in that factory.

5. If he *takes it into his head* to buy that car, he'll buy it, whatever we say.

6. The schoolmaster told the boy he would *get it in the neck* if he didn't *keep his nose to the grindstone*.

7. The policeman *kept an eye on* the suspicious-looking stranger.

8. I know that man. His name's *on the tip of my tongue*.

9. That secretary is too *smooth-tongued* for my liking.

10. I'm going to *put my foot down* now. I shan't do any more sentences.

Composition Exercises

1. Lucille couldn't think of anything more boring than a lesson on the parts of the body.

Write about eighty words on: (*a*) The most boring lesson I've ever been to (*be careful !*). (*b*) The most interesting lesson I've ever been to.

2. Write a story called *either* "The man who poked his nose into other people's business" *or* "A hair-breadth escape".

LESSON 36[1]

A Handful of Poems

(i)

Loveliest of trees, the cherry now
Is hung with bloom along the bough,
And stands about the woodland ride
Wearing white for Eastertide.

Now, of my three score years and ten,
Twenty will not come again,
And take from seventy springs a score,
It only leaves me fifty more.

And since to look at things in bloom
Fifty springs are little room,
About the woodlands I will go
To see the cherry hung with snow.

A. E. HOUSMAN (1859–1936).

---

[1] See special Glossary on p. 309 for words in this lesson.

(ii)

Leisure

What is this life if, full of care,
We have no time to stand and stare!

No time to stand beneath the boughs,
And stare as long as sheep and cows.

No time to see, when woods we pass,
Where squirrels hide their nuts in grass.

No time to see, in broad daylight,
Streams full of stars, like skies at night.

No time to turn at Beauty's glance,
And watch her feet, how they can dance.

.No time to wait till her mouth can
Enrich that smile her eyes began.

A poor life this if, full of care,
We have no time to stand and stare.

W. H. Davies (1871–1940).

(iii)

REQUIEM

Under the wide and starry sky,
 Dig the grave and let me lie.
Glad did I live and gladly die,
 And I laid me down with a will.

This be the verse you grave for me:
 Here he lies where he longed to be;
Home is the sailor, home from sea,
 And the hunter home from the hill.

R. L. STEVENSON (1850–1894).

(iv)

TO A LADY SEEN FROM THE TRAIN

O why do you walk through the fields in gloves,
Missing so much and so much ?
O fat white woman whom nobody loves,
Why do you walk through the fields in gloves,
When the grass is soft as the breast of doves
And shivering-sweet to the touch ?
O why do you walk through the fields in gloves,
Missing so much and so much ?

FRANCES CORNFORD (1886–   ).

(v)

O my Love's like a red, red rose
That's newly sprung in June:
O my Love's like the melody
That's sweetly played in tune.

As fair art thou, my bonny lass,
So deep in love am I:
And I will love thee still, my dear,
Till all the seas gang[1] dry:

Till all the seas gang dry, my dear,
And the rocks melt with the sun;
I will love thee still, my dear,
While the sands of life shall run.

And fare thee well, my only Love!
And fare thee well a while!
And I will come again, my Love,
Though it were ten thousand mile.

ROBERT BURNS (1759–1796).

[1] *gang* (Scottish)＝go. The spelling of some of the words has been
anglicised.

LONDON IN 1800

(vi)

UPON WESTMINSTER BRIDGE
September 3, 1802

Earth has not anything to show more fair:
  Dull would he be of soul who could pass by
  A sight so touching in its majesty:
This City now doth, like a garment, wear

The beauty of the morning: silent, bare,
  Ships, towers, domes, theatres, and temples lie
  Open unto the fields and to the sky,
All bright and glittering in the smokeless air.

Never did sun more beautifully steep
  In his first splendour valley, rock, or hill;
Ne'er saw I, never felt, a calm so deep!

The river glideth at his own sweet will:
Dear God! the very houses seem asleep;
  And all that mighty heart is lying still!

WILLIAM WORDSWORTH (1770–1850).

(vii)

TO A POET A THOUSAND YEARS HENCE

I who am dead a thousand years,
  And wrote this sweet archaic song,
Send you my words for messengers
  The way I shall not pass along.

I care not if you bridge the seas,
  Or ride secure the cruel sky,
Or build consummate palaces
  Of metal or of masonry.

But have you wine and music still,
  And statues and a bright-eyed love,
And foolish thoughts of good and ill,
  And prayers to them who sit above?

How shall we conquer? Like a wind
  That falls at eve our fancies blow,
And old Maeonides[1] the blind
  Said it three thousand years ago.

O friend unseen, unborn, unknown,
  Student of our sweet English tongue,
Read out my words at night, alone:
  I was a poet, I was young.

Since I can never see your face,
  And never shake you by the hand,
I send my soul through time and space
  To greet you. You will understand.

JAMES ELROY FLECKER (1884-1915).

[1] Homer.

LARK

SNAIL

(viii)

PIPPA'S SONG

The year's at the spring,
The day's at the morn;
Morning's at seven;
The hill-side's dew-pearled;
The lark's on the wing;
The snail's on the thorn;
God's in His Heaven—
All's right with the world.

ROBERT BROWNING (1812–1889).

(ix)

CROSSING THE BAR

Sunset and evening star,
And one clear call for me!
And may there be no moaning of the bar,
When I put out to sea,

But such a tide as moving seems asleep,
Too full for sound and foam
When that which drew from out the boundless deep
Turns again home.

Twilight and evening bell,
And after that the dark!
And may there be no sadness of farewell,
When I embark.

For though from out the bourne of Time and Place
The flood may bear me far,
I hope to see my Pilot face to face
When I have crossed the bar.

LORD TENNYSON (1809–1892).

*　　　*　　　*　　　*

HOB: I can't be bothered with poetry, unless it's comic poetry.

OLAF: Do you know any comic poetry, Hob?

HOB: Well, I know

There was a young lady of Niger,
Who went for a ride on a tiger,
They returned from the ride
With the lady inside
And a smile on the face of the tiger.

MR. PRIESTLEY: That's a limerick.

LUCILLE: What are limericks?

MR. PRIESTLEY: They are a form of comic verse. They generally begin: "There was a . . ."; they have five lines, three long ones (the first, second and fifth) with the same rhyme, and two short ones with another rhyme. There are hundreds of them in English. The most famous ones were those written by Edward Lear.[1]

FRIEDA: Could you tell us one of his?

MR. PRIESTLEY: Well, one of the best known is:

There was an old man with a beard,
Who said: "It is just as I feared!
Two owls and a hen,
Four larks and a wren,
Have all built their nests in my beard."

PEDRO: I know a limerick about a Japanese gentleman who had such a long name that it took several days to pronounce it.

[1] (1812–1888).

MR. PRIESTLEY: All limericks are not quite suitable for a class like this; but I know that one, and you can tell it quite safely.

PEDRO: Thank you, sir. It goes:

> There was a great man of Japan,
> Whose name on a Tuesday began;
>   It lasted through Sunday
>   Till midnight on Monday
> And sounded like stones in a can.

MR. PRIESTLEY: I don't think the limerick is to be found in any language except English. Neither is the Clerihew.

JAN: That's a strange word. Whatever is a Clerihew?

MR. PRIESTLEY: It's a form of comic verse invented by Edmund Clerihew Bentley.[1] A Clerihew has only four lines and is a sort of comic "biography". In fact Mr. Bentley called his book of Clerihews *Biography for Beginners*.

LUCILLE: I'd love to hear some of them.

MR. PRIESTLEY: Well, here's the opening one:

> The Art of Biography
> Is different from Geography.
> Geography is about maps,
> But Biography is about chaps.

FRIEDA: That's lovely. Do you know any more?

MR. PRIESTLEY: Well, here are two:

> What I like about Clive[2]
> Is that he is no longer alive.
> There's a great deal to be said
> For being dead.

[1] (1875-1956).
[2] Lord Clive (1725-1774). Conquered Bengal, founded British rule in India.

and

> Sir Christopher Wren[1]
> Said, "I am going to dine with some men.
> If anybody calls
> Say I'm designing St. Paul's."

LUCILLE: I saw a little poem a day or two ago about a boy called Jim. It reminded me of Hob. It went:

> "Pudding and pie"
> Said Jim, "Oh my!"
> "Which would you rather?"
> Said his father.
> "Both," said Jim.
> That's just like him.

HOB: It's a funny thing but I saw a little poem a day or two ago that reminded me of Lucille. It went:

> "She could dance till long past midnight,
> She could swim and she could run,
> She could row upon the river;
> And to climb, she thought, was fun.
>
> She'd play golf from morn till evening,
> Or tennis all day long,
> But she never touched the housework—
> Because she wasn't very strong."

[1] (1632–1723). England's greatest architect. Planned the rebuilding of St. Paul's Cathedral and fifty-two other churches in London after the Great Fire in 1666.

LESSON 37

The End of Another Year's Work

JAN, PEDRO, HOB

JAN: We've been studying here together for nearly three years now; doesn't time fly?

PEDRO: Yes. Another six months or so, and I shall be leaving Mr. Priestley. What are you thinking of doing when you leave, Jan?

JAN: Oh, I shall try to get a job in England, in an office, I expect, though I should hate it.

PEDRO: Why, isn't that what you really want to do?

JAN: No. I don't want that at all.

PEDRO: What would you like to do if you could please yourself?

JAN: I should like to be a doctor. I have always wanted that ever since I left school. I had planned to go to a university to study medicine, but that is out of the question now.

PEDRO: How is that; if you don't mind my asking?

JAN: Oh, I don't mind at all. The fact of the matter is, my father died three years ago and I can never hope to have enough money to pay for a university course—unless I can sell my factory in England.

HOB: What do you mean? Do you mean to say you own a factory in England?

JAN: Yes, worse luck. It happened like this. My father was an electrical engineer and he invented a new kind of electric lamp that would give more light than the old kind and use less current. He was doing very well with it in his own factory and then, about five years ago, an old friend of his, Antony Bruton, an Englishman whom he had been with at Cambridge, suggested that they should go into partnership together and build a place in England.

HOB: Antony Bruton captained England at cricket against Australia, didn't he? I've heard my Uncle Albert speak about him; he was a grand fellow.

PEDRO: Bruton lost his life when the *Alcestis* was shipwrecked.

JAN: How did you know that?

PEDRO: I knew Bruton. I was on that ship too, but I'll tell you about that some other time. What about your factory, Jan?

JAN: Well, Bruton and my father sank all their capital in building a big factory. It's a beautiful place with about four square miles of land round it. The only disadvantage is that there is no railway or road near it.

PEDRO: But, good heavens, I should have thought that would have been the first thing they would see about.

JAN: Yes, they should have made sure of that, but Bruton had been told on what he thought was absolutely trustworthy authority that the railway company were going to build a line running just past the factory. Well, they didn't. Their plans were changed just about the time the factory was finished, and there it stands all complete but empty and lifeless, miles from anywhere. My father and Bruton were ruined. My father worked himself to death to pay off the debt, and all I have in the world is about £200 and a factory that no one will buy, miles from anywhere.

HOB: Well, it may make your fortune yet; you never know.

JAN: Oh, no, Hob, there's no hope of that. It cost £50,000 to build, and I should think I was lucky if I were offered £5,000 for it.

HOB: I've got an idea!

JAN: What is it?

HOB: I'm not going to tell you just yet; it may come to nothing, but I want you to promise me that you will not sell that factory.

JAN: Unfortunately, I'm not likely to have the chance.

HOB: Never mind. Will you promise me that you will not sell without first telling me? It's really very important.

JAN: Very well, Hob, I promise, though I don't understand it at all.

HOB: Never mind; you will some day.[1] I must go now. I'll see you later; good-bye.

JAN: Good-bye. (*Hob goes out.*) I wonder what idea he has got in his head now.

PEDRO: He's a good-hearted fellow, but I've not much faith in any of his ideas. But never mind Hob,

[1] He does—in Book IV.

let's come back to you. Do you think that you would really like a doctor's life? Personally, I shouldn't like it at all.

JAN: There's nothing I should like better.

PEDRO: Wouldn't you find the work very tiring? You would be out all day six or seven days a week, and you would never be sure of getting a good night's sleep.

JAN: Oh, I know all that—but that wouldn't worry me; I like hard work.

PEDRO: How much do you think it would cost to do the training?

JAN: I don't quite know; three or four thousand pounds, perhaps. But it's no use talking about it any more; it can't happen now and I must get on with some other work.

PEDRO: I'm not so sure about that. Look here, I have much more money than I need, and if you would like the loan of the money, I should be very pleased to lend it to you. You could pay me back any time—so much a year when you are earning money—I shouldn't be in any hurry for it.

JAN: Pedro, I don't know how to thank you: it sounds too good to be true—but I can't take all that money from you.

PEDRO: Nonsense. I'm only too glad to be able to help you. Besides, you are not taking it from me; you are going to pay it all back. Of course, before we can do anything I shall have to see my lawyer, but I don't think there will be any difficulty at all.

JAN: If it could be arranged I should feel life was worth living again. I would work day and night to repay you.

PEDRO: Oh, I know you would; that's all right. Here's Mr. Priestley and the others; it's time for the lesson. Don't say a word about this to any of the others. And now let's go and see Mr. Priestley; he's waiting for us.

EXERCISES

I. *Use the following words and phrases in sentences:*

1. ever since
2. out of the question
3. the fact of the matter
4. current
5. into partnership
6. capital
7. disadvantage
8. authority
9. miles from anywhere
10. fortune
11. it's no use
12. faith
13. loan
14. eagerly
15. pay me back

II. *Use the following groups of words to make sentences.* You may add other words and change the order. You may have to change the tense of some of the verbs.

1. father, partnership, go, Antony Bruton, captain, at cricket.
2. like, doctor, want, school, leave.
3. never, money, hope, enough, that.
4. use, twice, light, give, half, current.
5. life, lose, wreck.
6. capital, sink, plan, factory, build.
7. beautiful, square, land, disadvantage, railway.
8. promise, want, sell, factory.

Composition Exercises

1. Tell the story of Jan's factory.
2. Jan wants to be a doctor. What do you want to be? Why?
3. Suppose someone you didn't know suggested that you went into a business partnership with them, what would you do?

TEST PAPER No. 3

I. *Rewrite the following sentences*, (a) *in the negative*, (b) *in the interrogative:*

1. You have three sisters.
2. They had many friends in France.
3. He often has a cup of tea in bed.
4. She has the tickets in her handbag.
5. Jan and Frieda have some friends in Wales.

II. *Use the following phrases in sentences.* You may use the verbs in any tense you like.

1. get rid of
2. in places
3. I'm tired of
4. round and round
5. any minute now
6. go in search of
7. to be struck by
8. not to be compared with
9. to be due to
10. at the edges
11. a waste of time
12. at thirty miles an hour
13. it's no use
14. out of the question
15. ever since

III. *In the following sentences,* (a) *put in the correct form of* do, (b) *say whether* do *is being used as a "full" or as a "special" verb.*

1. He — that exercise yesterday.
2. Have you — what I told you?
3. He — not listen to what I say.
4. Andrew ought to — better than that.
5. — you like cabbage? No, I — .
6. — you give the gardener his money?
7. I am — my best.
8. He — not go to Switzerland after all.
9. He must — this exercise again.
10. The soldiers have — their duty bravely.

IV. *Complete these sentences in your own words:*

1. I suppose we ought . . .
2. During the next four hundred years . . .
3. I have always wanted . . .
4. I'm sure you will . . .
5. While I am in England . . .
6. I'm no good at . . .
7. I never saw such . . .
8. I never bother about . . .
9. I liked the story about . . .
10. If you don't do better than that . . .

V. *Rewrite the following sentences* (a) *in the negative,* (b) *in the interrogative:*

1. His house needs painting.
2. They need more money.
3. Olaf needed a new coat.

Answer the following questions:

4. Need you go now? Yes, I — .
5. Who needn't work tomorrow? George — .
6. Need I go to London? Yes, you — .
7. Does he need to make such a noise? No, he — .

VI. *Rewrite the following piece and put in capital letters and punctuation:*

may i have the bill now asked mr jones having finished a poor lunch the waitress came slowly over what did you have she asked badly cooked meat hard peas old potatoes and dry bread that ll be three and six said the waitress oh and i had a glass of water which was quite nice added jones three and eight came the reply

VII. (a) *Give in one word the meaning of each of the following words or phrases.* The number of letters in the word is given in brackets after it. *Write your answers one under the other and the first letter of each word will give you the name of a famous English author.* (b) *When you have found his name give the titles of three of his works.*

(*a*) an act which breaks the laws of God (3)
(*b*) the back part of the foot (4)
(*c*) old (7)
(*d*) monarch (4)
(*e*) a number of different countries ruled by one chief government (6)
(*f*) he takes care of sheep (8)
(*g*) a number of persons going along in a line (10)
(*h*) to have happiness in (5)
(*i*) to say a thing is good (7)
(*j*) to decide (7)
(*k*) full of desire, very anxious to (do) (12)

VIII. *Answer these questions in the negative:*

1. Dare you tell her what you think of her?
2. Didn't you use to know a girl called Belinda?
3. Did you have a good journey?
4. Used you to live in Brussels?
5. Are you used to that typewriter now?
6. Need I put on a clean collar?
7. Ought he to travel without a ticket?
8. Will he dare to return to Brazil?
9. Have you done what I told you?
10. Did she dare to do it again?

IX. *Write about 250 words on one of the following:*

1. Wales.
2. An ideal holiday.
3. A quick way to make money.
4. The man in history (or literature) I admire most.

X. *Read the following passage carefully and answer the questions below:*

The old woman told me the house had been built in 1595 and this was not hard to believe. The small windows, the uneven floors, the roughly-made doors and an ancient oak desk had obviously all seen the passing of many generations. In fact I learned later that at that desk a certain parson, who lived in the house half a century after it had been built, had written a bad-tempered diary, blaming his and the country's misfortunes on the government, and sorrowing over the passing of the "good old days". The diary reminded me of some present-day letters to *The Times*, in which all that is present is bad and all that is past is good.

I was fascinated by the great open fireplace, over whose roaring log fire pigs were roasted. It has occurred to me that the parson would have had more to complain about if, instead of a generous helping of roast pork, he had been served with some of the meat we eat today.

The old woman, who was showing me round, seemed almost as ancient as the house. She took little notice of me; I was merely another "gentleman from London" who would look round her beloved house and then decide not to have it because there was no electricity, or no water, or because it was too far to walk from there to the village. But she was wrong. I had decided otherwise.

(1) *In about what year did the parson live in the house?*

(2) *Why did the writer call the parson's diary "bad-tempered"?*

(3) *What is "The Times"?*

(4) *What did the writer think would not have pleased the parson if he had lived today?*

(5) *What was the writer doing in the house?*

(6) *What disadvantages of living in an old house are suggested in this piece?*

(7) *Give another word or phrase of similar meaning to that in which the following words or phrases are used in the passage: (a) uneven, (b) diary, (c) reminded me of, (d) I was fascinated, (e) complain.*

(8) *In not more than 80 words, describe what you imagine the outside and the garden of this house looked like.*

Good-bye

Mr. Priestley's Study. MR. PRIESTLEY AND ALL THE STUDENTS ARE THERE.

MR. PRIESTLEY: Well, here we are at the end of another year's work, and it's "good-bye" for a while.

PEDRO: I'm very sorry we have to finish now; I've thoroughly enjoyed our lessons together—and I'm sure, too, everyone else has [OTHERS: "Hear, hear!"], and I'm looking forward eagerly to next year's work.

MR. PRIESTLEY: And it is going to be a very full, busy and, I hope, enjoyable year.

But now, till next year, it's good-bye, and a most pleasant holiday.

*   *   *   *

Mr. Priestley Gets a Surprise

TIME: *Midnight.* MR. *and* MRS. PRIESTLEY (*and* SALLY) *are sitting by the fire.*

MR. PRIESTLEY: Well, Mary, my students have all gone; and, do you know, I'm quite sorry to lose them.

MRS. PRIESTLEY: I'm sure you are. They are the nicest group of students that you have ever had.

MR. PRIESTLEY: By the way, I had a most embarrassing experience this afternoon. I thought all my students had gone away, and I was just going into my study when I saw that Jan and Frieda were there. Their backs were towards me, and I heard Jan say, "Frieda", and she said, "Jan", and the next moment she was in his arms. It was most embarrassing for me.

MRS. PRIESTLEY: What did you do?

MR. PRIESTLEY: Well, my dear, I didn't quite know what to do, so I just closed the door very quietly and came away on tiptoe.

MRS. PRIESTLEY: I should hope you did!

MR. PRIESTLEY: I was never so surprised in all my life. I hadn't guessed ——

MRS. PRIESTLEY: Charles Priestley, you may be a clever man and a good teacher and all that, but I sometimes think you don't see the simplest thing that is taking place under your very nose.

MR. PRIESTLEY: What, do you mean to say you knew Jan was in love with Frieda?

MRS. PRIESTLEY: Of course I did. A babe could have seen it; and I must say I'm very glad that he has told her at last. She is a charming girl, and they ought to be very happy together.

MR. PRIESTLEY: Well, well, well, you surprise me.

MRS. PRIESTLEY: Come along, it's after twelve o'clock and time both of us were in bed.

PRONOUNCING VOCABULARY
OF ESSENTIAL ENGLISH BOOK III

Each student should get a small notebook, mark it out into sections alphabetically and, when he meets a new word, he should write it down in the proper section and add the translation.

abbreviation
    [əbri:vi′eiʃ(ə)n]
ability [ə′biliti]
accent [′æksnt]
accept [ək′sept]
accompany
    [ə′kʌmpəni]
accuse [ə′kju:z]
accustomed
    [ə′kʌstəmd]
activity [æk′tiviti]
actually [′æktju(ə)li]
administrative
    [əd′ministrətiv]
admiration
    [ædmə′reiʃ(ə)n]
admire [əd′maiə]
admit [əd′mit]
adopt [ə′dɔpt]
advanced [əd′va:nst]
advantage
    [əd′va:ntidʒ]
affairs [ə′fɛəz]
affect [ə′fekt]
afford [ə′fɔ:d]
agitated [′ædʒiteitid]
agricultural
    [ægri′kʌltʃərəl]
alphabetical
    [ælfə′betikl]
altar [′ɔ:ltə]
ambassador
    [æm′bæsədə]
angel [′eindʒl]
announce [ə′nauns]
announcer
    [ə′naunsə]

annoyed [ə′nɔid]
ant [ænt]
appear [ə′piə]
appearance
    [ə′piərəns]
applause [ə′plɔ:z]
appoint [ə′pɔint]
appreciate
    [ə′pri:ʃieit]
approve [ə′pru:v]
archer [′a:tʃə]
architecture
    [′a:kitektʃə]
armed [′a:md]
armour [′a:mə]
arrow [′ærou]
art [a:t]
ashamed [ə′ʃeimd]
associate [ə′souʃieit]
atom [′ætəm]
attack [ə′tæk]
attempt [ə′tem(p)t]
attend [ə′tend]
authority [ɔ:′θɔriti]
avoid [ə′vɔid]
awe [ɔ:]

background
    [′bækgraund]
balcony [′bælkəni]
bald [bɔ:ld]
bar [ba:]
barber [′ba:bə]
bard [ba:d]
bare [bɛə]
battle [′bætl]

beam (n.) [bi:m]
bear (v.) [bɛə]
bench [benʃ]
bet [bet]
betray [bi′trei]
billiards [′biljədz]
biography
    [bai′ɔgrəfi]
bishop [′biʃəp]
blameless [′bleimlis]
blood [blʌd]
bloodstained
    [′blʌdsteind]
blot (v.) [blɔt]
boar [bɔ:]
bolt [boult]
bomb [bɔm]
boots [bu:ts]
boring [′bɔ:riŋ]
bother [′bɔðə]
bottom [′bɔt(ə)m]
boundary
    [′baundəri]
bow (n.) [bou]
bow (v.) [bau]
bowl [′boul]
branch [bra:nʃ]
bravely [′breivli]
breastplate
    [′brestpleit]
brilliant [′briljənt]
broad [brɔ:d]
brush [brʌʃ]
burden [′bə:dn]
burgled [′bə:gld]
bust (n.) [bʌst]
button [′bʌtn]

cage [keidʒ]

camp [kæmp]

candidate ['kændidit]

captain ['kæptin]

captive ['kæptiv]

careless ['kɛəlis]

carpenter ['kɑːpintə]

castle ['kɑːsl]

cathedral [kə'θiːdr(ə)l]

celebrate ['selibreit]

centre ['sentə]

century ['sentʃəri]

challenge ['tʃælindʒ]

chancellor ['tʃɑːnsilə]

chapel ['tʃæp(ə)l]

chaps [tʃæps]

characteristic [kæriktə'ristik]

cheek [tʃiːk]

cheer [tʃiə]

cherry ['tʃeri]

chieftain ['tʃiːftən]

chimney ['tʃimni]

choir ['kwaiə]

circumstances ['səːk(ə)mstənsiz]

citizen ['sitizn]

claim [kleim]

climate ['klaimit]

colloquial [kə'loukwiəl]

colonel ['kəːnl]

colony ['kɔləni]

combine [kəm'bain]

comfort ['kʌmfət]

comic ['kɔmik]

command [kə'mɑːnd]

committee [kə'miti]

companion [kəm'pænjən]

compete [kəm'piːt]

competition [kɔmpi'tiʃ(ə)n]

competitor [kəm'petitə]

complaint [kəm'pleint]

complicated ['kɔmplikeitid]

compulsion [kəm'pʌlʃ(ə)n]

compulsory [kəm'pʌlsəri]

concern [kən'səːn]

condemn [kən'dem]

condition [kən'diʃ(ə)n]

confidence ['kɔnfidəns]

confirmation [kɔnfə'meiʃ(ə)n]

congratulations [kəngrætju'leiʃ(ə)ns]

connect [kə'nekt]

conquer ['kɔŋkə]

consider [kən'sidə]

console [kən'soul]

constantly ['kɔnstəntli]

construction [kən'strʌkʃ(ə)n]

continuity [kɔnti'njuːiti]

contradict [kɔntrə'dikt]

contrast ['kɔntrɑːst]

control [kən'troul]

convenient [kən'viːniənt]

corresponding [kɔris'pɔndiŋ]

cosy ['kouzi]

countryside ['kʌntrisaid]

cradle ['kreidl]

cremate [kri'meit]

critical ['kritikl]

criticise ['kritisaiz]

cross-eyed ['krɔsaid]

crown [kraun]

cruel ['kruəl]

culture ['kʌltʃə]

current ['kʌrənt]

cushion ['kuʃ(ə)n]

daffodil ['dæfədil]

daresay ['dɛəsei]

dash (v.) [dæʃ]

debate [di'beit]

decision [di'siʒ(ə)n]

declare [di'klɛə]

deed [diːd]

deep [diːp]

defeat [di'fiːt]

defend [di'fend]

definition [defi'niʃ(ə)n]

degree [di'griː]

delight [di'lait]

delightful [di'laitful]

deny [di'nai]

descend [di'send]

design [di'zain]

detail ['diːteil]

develop [di'veləp]

devoted [di'voutid]

dialect ['daiəlekt]

diary ['daiəri]

differ ['difə]

disadvantage [disəd'va:ntidʒ]
disappear [disə'piə]
disappointed [disə'pɔintid]
disciple [di'saipl]
discipline ['disiplin]
discover [dis'kʌvə]
discuss [dis'kʌs]
disgrace [dis'greis]
distant ['distənt]
disturb [dis'tə:b]
don [dɔn]
doorway ['dɔ:wei]
drag [dræg]
dreadful ['dredful]
dream [dri:m]
drip [drip]

eagerly ['i:gəli]
educated ['edju(:)keitid]
education [edju(:)'keiʃ(ə)n]
effect [i'fekt]
egg-timer ['egtaimə]
element ['elimənt]
eloquently ['eləkwəntli]
embarrassing [im'bærəsiŋ]
emphasis ['emfəsis]
emphasise ['emfəsaiz]
emphatic [im'fætik]
entrance ['entrəns]
escape [is'keip]
event [i'vent]
evil ['i:vl]
examine [ig'zæmin]

excursion [iks'kə:ʃ(ə)n]
exist [ig'zist]
expectation [ekspek'teiʃ(ə)n]
expel [iks'pel]
expenditure [iks'penditʃə]
experience [iks'piəriəns]
experimental [iksperi'mentl]
expert ['ekspə:t]
extended [iks'tendid]
extensive [iks'tensiv]

fair (n.) [fɛə]
faith [feiθ]
fame [feim]
fascinating ['fæsineitiŋ]
feast [fi:st]
feather ['feðə]
feature ['fi:tʃə]
feelings ['fi:liŋs]
fertile ['fə:tail]
festival ['festivl]
fiercely ['fiəsli]
film [film]
fine (n. & v.) [fain]
fix [fiks]
float [flout]
flood [flʌd]
footsteps ['futsteps]
forbid [fə'bid]
force (v.) [fɔ:s]
forcibly ['fɔ:sibli]
forehead ['fɔrid]
forgive [fə'giv]
formal ['fɔ:ml]

fort [fɔ:t]
foundations [faun'deiʃ(ə)nz]
fountain pen ['fauntin pen]
frontier ['frʌntjə]
fulfil [ful'fil]
fur [fə:]
fuss [fʌs]

gap [gæp]
garage ['gæra:ʒ] ['gæridʒ]
generation [dʒenə'reiʃ(ə)n]
generous ['dʒenərəs]
genuine ['dʒenjuin]
geography [dʒi'ɔgrəfi]
gift [gift]
gigantic [dʒai'gæntik]
glance [gla:ns]
God [gɔd]
govern ['gʌvən]
gown [gaun]
grace [greis]
gradually ['grædju(ə)li]
grain [grein]
grasshopper ['gra:shɔpə]
grave (adj.) [greiv]
grave (n.) [greiv]
greengrocer ['gri:ngrousə]
grindstone ['graindstoun]
guardian ['ga:djən]
guess [ges]

habitual [hə'bitju(ə)l]
hairbreadth ['hɛəbredθ]
handful ['hændful]
hare [hɛə]
harm [hɑːm]
harp [hɑːp]
hastily ['heistili]
heal [hiːl]
heathen ['hiːð(ə)n]
helmet ['helmit]
hesitate ['heziteit]
hide [haid]
hill [hil]
hole [houl]
holy ['houli]
homesickness ['housmiknis]
horn [hɔːn]
horrible ['hɔribl]
horrid ['hɔrid]
horrify ['hɔrifai]
housewife ['hauswaif]
huge [hjuːdʒ]
human ['hjuːmən]
hymn [him]

idiomatic [idiə'mætik]
imagination [imædʒi'neiʃ(ə)n]
imply [im'plai]
impress [im'pres]
imprison [im'prizn]
incline [in'klain]
include [in'kluːd]
income ['inkəm]
independent [indi'pendənt]

indirect [indi'rekt]
individuality [individju'æliti]
inflection [in'flekʃ(ə)n]
influence ['influəns]
informal [in'fɔːməl]
inhabit [in'hæbit]
inheritance [in'heritəns]
inn [in]
inner ['inə]
innocent ['inəsənt]
insist [in'sist]
insult (n.) ['insʌlt]
insult (v.) [in'sʌlt]
interview ['intəvjuː]
intonation [intə'neiʃ(ə)n]
invader [in'veidə]
invitation [invi'teiʃ(ə)n]
invite [in'vait]
irregular [i'regjulə]
item ['aitem]

jealous ['dʒeləs]
jelly ['dʒeli]
jolly ['dʒɔli]
justify ['dʒʌstifai]

kneel [niːl]
knighthood ['naithud]

labourer ['leibərə]
ladder ['lædə]

lake [leik]
lame [leim]
lark [lɑːk]
law [lɔː]
lawyer ['lɔːjə]
lazy ['leizi]
leader ['liːdə]
leather ['leðə]
lecture ['lektʃə]
leek [liːk]
lemon ['lemən]
lemonade [lemən'eid]
level ['levl]
lieutenant [lef'tenənt] [luː'tenənt]
lifeless ['laiflis]
lips [lips]
lively ['laivli]
local ['loukl]
lock [lɔk]
log [lɔg]
longing ['lɔŋiŋ]
loss [lɔs]

magnificent [mæg'nifisənt]
maiden ['meidn]
main [mein]
majesty ['mædʒisti]
major ['meidʒə]
majority [mə'dʒɔriti]
map [mæp]
martyr ['mɑːtə]
master ['mɑːstə]
mathematics [mæθi'mætiks]
mayor ['mɛə]

meantime ['miːntaim]

meanwhile ['miːnwail]

mechanic [mi'kænik]

medical ['medikl]

medieval [medi'iːvl]

melt [melt]

memorial [mi'mɔːriəl]

memory ['meməri]

merely ['miəli]

merrily ['merili]

message ['mesidʒ]

messenger ['mesindʒə]

metal ['metl]

mid-way ['mid wei]

mingling ['miŋgliŋ]

minister ['ministə]

miraculous [mi'rækjuləs]

misprint ['misprint]

mist [mist]

misunderstanding [misʌndə'stændiŋ]

monarch ['mɔnək]

monk [mʌŋk]

monument ['mɔnjumənt]

moreover [mɔː'rouvə]

mountaineering [maunti'niəriŋ]

mulberry ['mʌlbəri]

mule [mjuːl]

murder ['məːdə]

musician [mjuː'ziʃ(ə)n]

mystery ['mist(ə)ri]

napkin ['næpkin]

narrow ['nærou]

native ['neitiv]

nature ['neitʃə]

navy ['neivi]

neat [niːt]

necessity [ni'sesiti]

needle ['niːdl]

needless ['niːdlis]

neighbourhood ['neibəhud]

nest [nest]

noble ['noubl]

nobleman ['noublmən]

notebook ['noutbuk]

nurse [nəːs]

oak [ouk]

objection [əb'dʒekʃ(ə)n]

obligation [ɔbli'geiʃ(ə)n]

observation [ɔbsə'veiʃən]

observe [əb'zəːv]

obstacle ['ɔbstikl]

occupation [ɔkju'peiʃ(ə)n]

occupied ['ɔkjupaid]

odd [ɔd]

offence [ə'fens]

offer ['ɔfə]

off-hand [ɔf'hænd]

official [ə'fiʃl]

old-fashioned ['ould'fæʃ(ə)nd]

omit [ou'mit]

organisation [ɔːgənai'zeiʃ(ə)n]

organise ['ɔːgənaiz]

originally [ə'ridʒinəli]

overturn [ouvə'təːn]

owl [aul]

palace ['pælis]

pale [peil]

parson ['pɑːsn]

partnership ['pɑːtnəʃip]

passage ['pæsidʒ]

passionate ['pæʃənit]

pause [pɔːz]

pea [piː]

peak [piːk]

peculiar [pi'kjuːliə]

peculiarity [pikjuːli'æriti]

perfection [pə'fekʃ(ə)n]

permanent ['pəːmənənt]

personal ['pəːsənl]

philosophy [fi'lɔsəfi]

photograph ['foutəgrɑːf]

pick [pik]

pilot ['pailət]

pin [pin]

pink [piŋk]

pity ['piti]

plant [plɑːnt]

plot (v.) [plɔt]

political [pə'litikl]

politician [pəli'tiʃ(ə)n]

porch [pɔːtʃ]

portion ['pɔːʃn]
portrait ['pɔːtrit]
position [pə'ziʃ(ə)n]
possess [pə'zes]
possible ['pɔsibl]
pour [pɔː]
power ['pauə]
pray [prei]
prayer ['prɛə]
precious ['preʃəs]
preliminary
    [pri'liminəri]
preparation
    [prepə'reiʃ(ə)n]
prepare [pri'pɛə]
priest [priːst]
Prime Minister
    [praim 'ministə]
printing-press
    ['printiŋ pres]
procession
    [prə'seʃ(ə)n]
prompt [prɔmpt]
public ['pʌblik]
publish ['pʌbliʃ]
puff [pʌf]
punctuation
    [pʌnktju'eiʃ(ə)n]
punishment
    ['pʌniʃmənt]
pure [pjuə]
purple ['pəːpl]
purpose ['pəːpəs]

quarrel ['kwɔr(ə)l]
queer ['kwiə]

rage [reidʒ]
ragged ['rægid]

rank [ræŋk]
rare [rɛə]
rate [reit]
reality [riː'æliti]
rebel (n.) ['rebl]
rebel (v.) [ri'bel]
rebellious [ri'beliəs]
reduce [ri'djuːs]
refuge ['refjuːdʒ]
regular ['regjulə]
reign [rein]
relative ['relətiv]
religion [ri'lidʒən]
religious [ri'lidʒəs]
remove [ri'muːv]
reported [ri'pɔːtid]
reputation
    [repjuː'teiʃ(ə)n]
request [ri'kwest]
require [ri'kwaiə]
rescue ['reskjuː]
research [ri'səːtʃ]
resist [ri'zist]
resolve [ri'zɔlv]
retreat [ri'triːt]
rhyme [raim]
rights [raits]
riot [raiət]
robe [roub]
romantic
    [rou'mæntik]
roundabout
    ['raundəbaut]
row (v.) [rou]
rugby ['rʌgbi]
ruin [ruin]
rush [rʌʃ]

sacrifice ['sækrifais]
saint [seint]

sand-glass
    ['sænd glɑːs]
sauce [sɔːs]
scarcely ['skɛəsli]
scatter [s'kætə]
scent [sent]
scholarly ['skɔləli]
scholarship
    ['skɔləʃip]
schoolmaster
    ['skuːlmɑːstə]
science ['saiəns]
screw [skruː]
screw-driver
    ['skruːdraivə]
scrub [skrʌb]
sculptor ['skʌlptə]
search [səːtʃ]
secretly ['siːkritli]
seize [siːz]
self-governing
    [self'gʌvəniŋ]
selfish ['selfiʃ]
sergeant
    ['sɑːdʒ(ə)nt]
sermon ['səːmən]
service ['səːvis]
set [set]
settle ['setl]
shameful ['ʃeimful]
shamrock ['ʃæmrɔk]
share [ʃɛə]
sheath [ʃiːθ]
shelter ['ʃeltə]
shepherd ['ʃepəd]
sherry ['ʃeri]
shield [ʃiːld]
shore [ʃɔː]
should [ʃud]
shoulder ['ʃouldə]
sight [sait]

significant ['sig'nifikənt]
sign-post ['sainpoust]
silk [silk]
sin (v.) [sin]
sink [siŋk]
skill [skil]
slave [sleiv]
slip [slip]
slope [sloup]
society [sə'saiəti]
soloist ['soulouist]
soul [soul]
sour ['sauə]
space [speis]
spanner ['spænə]
speech [spi:tʃ]
speed [spi:d]
spill [spil]
split [split]
spread [spred]
stage [steidʒ]
staircase ['stɛəkeis]
stake [steik]
standard ['stændəd]
stare [stɛə]
statesman ['steitsmən]
statue ['stætju:]
steady ['stedi]
steam [sti:m]
stem [stem]
store (v.) [stɔ:]
stream [stri:m]
stress [stres]
strike [straik]
stroke [strouk]
struggle ['strʌgl]
subjection [səb'dʒekʃ(ə)n]

succeed [sək'si:d]
successor [sək'sesə]
suggest [sə'dʒest]
support [sə'pɔ:t]
surround [sə'raund]
swallow ['swɔlou]
swear [swɛə]
swing (n.) [swiŋ]
sword [sɔ:d]

tax [tæks]
telegraph ['teligrɑ:f]
tent [tent]
term [tə:m]
thatched ['θætʃt]
theory ['θiəri]
thistle ['θisl]
thread [θred]
threaten ['θretn]
thrifty ['θrifti]
throne [θroun]
throughout [θru:'aut]
thrust [θrʌst]
thunder ['θʌndə]
tide [taid]
tidy ['taidi]
tiger ['taigə]
tiny ['taini]
tiptoe ['tiptou]
toe [tou]
tone [toun]
tools [tu:lz]
torn [tɔ:n]
tower ['tauə]
toy [tɔi]
trace [treis]
tradition [trə'diʃ(ə)n]

traitor ['treitə]
trembling ['trembliŋ]
tremendous [tri'mendəs]
trial ['traiəl]
tribe [traib]
trip (n.) [trip]
trumpet ['trʌmpit]
trustworthy ['trʌstwə:ði]
tune [tju:n]
tutor ['tju:tə]
typically ['tipikəli]

ugly ['ʌgli]
undergraduate [ʌndə'grædjuət]
underneath [ʌndə'ni:θ]
undoubtedly [ʌn'dautidli]
uneasy [ʌn'i:zi]
ungrateful [ʌn'greitful]
unite [ju:'nait]
unknown [ʌn'noun]
unless [ən'les]
unlike [ʌn'laik]
unspoken [ʌn'spouk(ə)n]
upon [ə'pɔn]
upset [ʌp'set]
urgent ['ə:dʒənt]
usage ['ju:zidʒ]

vacation [və'keiʃ(ə)n]
valuable ['væljuəbl]

variety [vəˈraiəti]
various [ˈvɛəriəs]
veins [veinz]
verse [vəːs]
view [vjuː]
villain [ˈvilən]
vision [ˈviʒ(ə)n]
volume [ˈvɔljum]
vow [vau]
voyage [ˈvɔiidʒ]

wagon [ˈwæg(ə)n]
war [wɔː]
weave [wiːv]
whisky [ˈwiski]
whisper [ˈwispə]
whole-hearted
     [houlˈhɑːtid]
widespread
     [ˈwaidspred]
winding [ˈwaindiŋ]

wing [wiŋ]
wipe [waip]
witty [ˈwiti]
wooden [ˈwudn]
worship [ˈwəːʃip]
worthless
     [ˈwəːθlis]
would [wud]
wreck [rek]
wren [ren]

GLOSSARY FOR LESSON 36

As most of the new words in this lesson are " poetic " or part of a special rather than a general vocabulary, they are given here as a separate list. With the more unusual words a simple definition is given.

archaic [ɑːˈkeiik] = very old; no longer used.
bloom [bluːm] = flowers; blossoms.
bonny [ˈbɔni] = beautiful. The usual meaning is "pretty; healthy looking".
bough [bau] = large branch of a tree.
boundless [ˈbaundlis] = without end or limit.
bourne [buən] = bounds, limits.
chaps [tʃæps] = men (*slang*).
consummate [ˈkənˈsʌmit] = perfect.
dew [djuː] = small drops of water formed on cool objects after the sun goes down.
dome [doum] = large rounded roof.
dove [dʌv] = bird; kind of pigeon.
Eastertide [ˈiːstətaid] = Eastertime.
embark [imˈbɑːk] = go on board a ship.
enrich [inˈritʃ] = make rich.
foam [foum] = mass of white bubbles made by waves breaking.
garment [ˈgɑːmənt] = article of dress.
glideth [ˈglaidəθ] = poetic form of *glides*, i.e. moves smoothly and easily.
glitter [ˈglitə] = shine; send out a bright light.
leisure [ˈleʒə] = time not given to work.
masonry [ˈmeisənri] = stonework.
melody [ˈmelədi] = tune.

mighty ['maiti] = great and strong.

moaning ['mouniŋ] = sound of sadness.

owl [aul] = bird that flies at night.

requiem ['rekwiem] = music for the dead.

score [skɔ:] = twenty.

secure [si'kjuə] = safe.

shiver ['ʃivə] = tremble; *shivering-sweet* = so sweet it makes you tremble.

snail [sneil] *(see picture, p. 285)*.

splendour ['splendə] = magnificence; beauty; great brightness.

squirrel ['skwirəl] *(see picture, p. 280)*.

steep *(verb)* [sti:p] = soak, wet through.

temple ['templ] = building used for worship.

thorn [θɔ:n] = sharp point on a plant, e.g. rose.   But here *thorn* more likely means "haw*thorn* tree".

twilight ['twailait] = half-light just before and after sunset.

wren [ren] = small singing bird.

INDEX